Screen Shots

Creating a

Local Network

with Windows 95/98

Creating a
Local Network
with Windows 95/98

Luc Chataignier

CASSELL&CO

First published, revised and adapted, in the United Kingdom in 2000 by Hachette UK

© English Translation Hachette UK 2000
© Hachette Livre: Marabout Informatique 1999

English translation by Prose Unlimited and Dominique Laloux
Concept and editorial direction: Ghéorghïi Vladimirovitch Grigorieff
Additional research and editorial assistance: Chris Habberjam, Colette Holden, Andy Armitage, Jane Eady, Johan Rinchard and John Cardinal.

A CIP catalogue for this book is available from the British Library

Trademarks/Registered Trademarks

Computer hardware and software brand names mentioned in this book are protected by their respective trademarks and acknowledged. Every effort has been made to make this book as complete and accurate as possible, but the publisher and author cannot accept any responsibility for any loss or inconvenience sustained by any reader as a result of this book's information or advice.

ISBN 1 84202 041 2

Designed by Graph'M
Layout by B. Fabrot
Typeset in Humanist 521
Printed and bound by Graficas Estella, Spain

Hachette UK
Cassell & Co
The Orion Publishing Group
Wellington House
London
WC2R 0BB

Web site: www.marabout.com/Cassell

Contents

How to use this book

Welcome to this visual guide. It explains how to carry out some one hundred or so operations, ranging from the simple to the more complex, in a clear and methodical manner.

The book is divided into thematic chapters, which are in turn divided into sections. Each section deals with a separate topic and explains its many facets and uses, as well as detailing all related commands.

The orange 'Checklist' bookmarks that appear throughout the book contain lists of the procedures you must follow in order to complete a given task successfully. The accompanying screen shots have arrows pointing to certain parts of the screen. When the points in the checklist are numbered, they correspond directly with these numbered green arrows. When the points in the bookmarks bear letters they do not relate directly to the arrows, but simply provide additional useful information. When the arrows pointing to the screen are orange they give information on a particular feature, whilst the red arrows alert you of a possible danger, such as a button to avoid pressing at all costs!

In addition to illustrations of relevant screen shots as they should appear if instructions have been followed correctly, the Screen Shots series also features 'Tips' boxes and 'light-bulb' features that will help you get the most out of the programs. Shortcut keys are useful ways of saving time for frequently used commands. The 'Tips' boxes give handy time-saving hints, while the light-bulb features provide additional information by presenting an associated command, option or a particular type of use for the command.

Happy reading

Introduction

Networks allow **PCs** (and also minicomputers, workstations and mainframes) to communicate. Wide area networks (**WAN**s) like the Internet link computers on an international scale, while local area networks (**LAN**s) connect machines in the same local area. The latter are much faster than the former.

Two or more **PCs** can be connected through a **LAN**. The **PCs** will then be able to access the same drives or selected folders, making it possible to share and to save documents centrally. You will no longer need a **CD-ROM**, zip or jazz drive for each computer, as one single unit can be shared by all **PCs**. Similarly, regardless of the machine a printer is connected to, you will be able to access it from any other **PC** through the **LAN**.

Connecting **PCs** in a **LAN** is not expensive. All you need is a card – or Network Adapter – in each **PC**, cables and software that is available from the Windows 95/98 **CD-ROM**. Depending on the type of network chosen, you may also need a special device, the hub.

A local area network that allows **PCs** to share their printers and the contents of their hard drives, is called a peer-to-peer network. They are inexpensive and easy to configure and install. This book shows you how.

If you are not familiar with local networks, start with the first chapter, 'Understanding local area networks', for an introduction to **LAN**s for Windows 95/98.

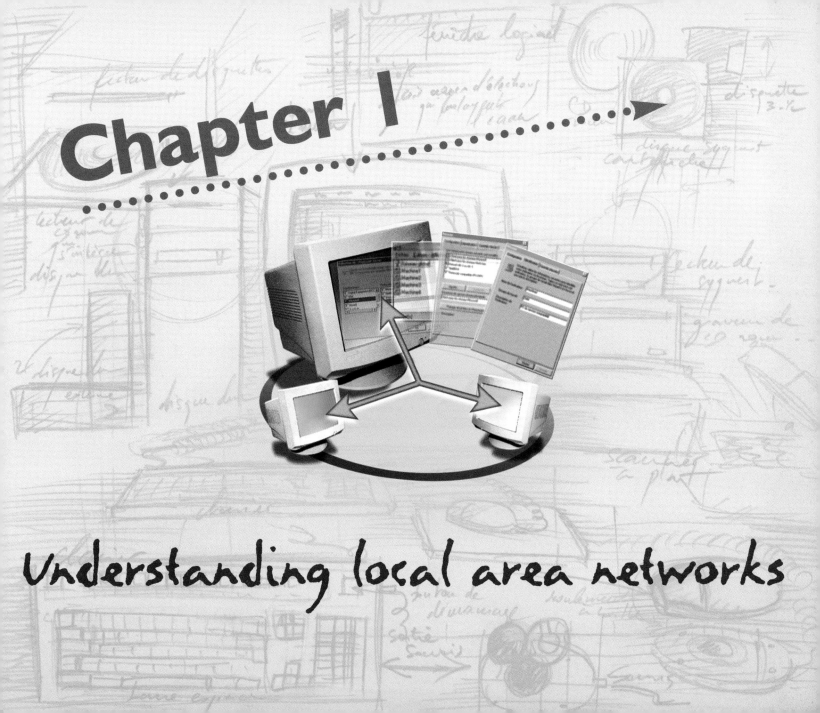

Chapter 1

Understanding local area networks

What is a local area network?

A LAN connects PCs through specal electric cables or (more expensive) optical fibres. The machines concerned are usually located in a limited geographical area (which is why we call it a 'local area' network). In this chapter we illustrate this using a simple diagram.

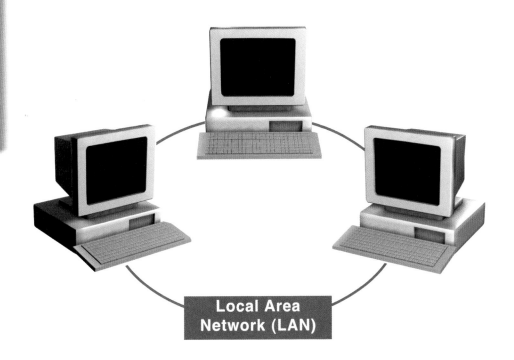

Local Area Network (LAN)

Some advantages of LANs:

- Hard disks, removable units, CD-ROMs and the printers of each PC can be shared with other PCs. In some cases, other resources, such as fax/modems or Internet connections, can also be shared, either directly or through the use of additional software or hardware.

- Access to messaging services, and to related features and products (attachments, forms etc.).

- Possibility of saving documents centrally, i.e. on a single machine.

- Facilitation of team work.

A local area network may include all kinds of machines

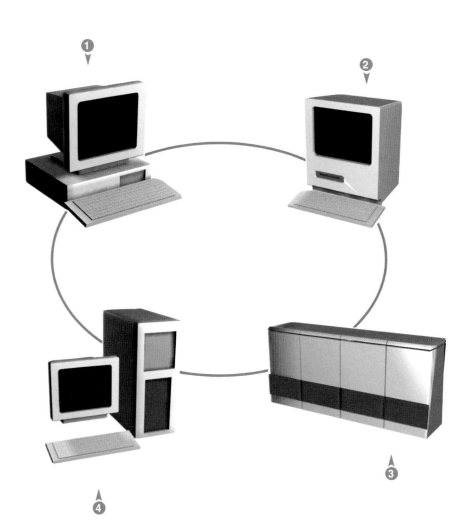

A LAN may include all kinds of machines.

1 PC.

2 Macintosh.

3 Medium-sized and large systems (mainframes).

4 UNIX workstation.

To connect two or more LANs, lines are leased from a telecom operator. The most common line used is called an ISDN. The network is then called a *wide area network* or WAN.

A Simplified view of a wide area network

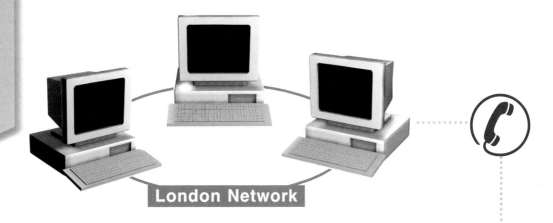

London Network

The Internet is not a WAN because it does not belong to a single company or organisation, as is the case of a standard LAN or a WAN. A company can be connected continuously (round the clock) to the Internet through specific hardware called a router (sometimes expensive and complex to maintain) subject to high non-recurrent and recurrent fees. An individual can connect to the Internet simply through a modem or an ISDN adapter, via an Internet service provider (ISP).

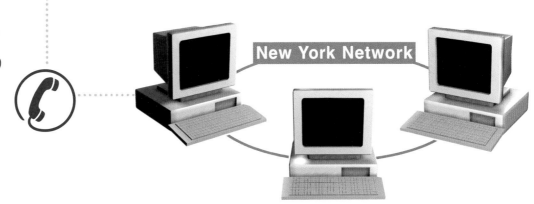

New York Network

Sharing resources in a local area network: general principles

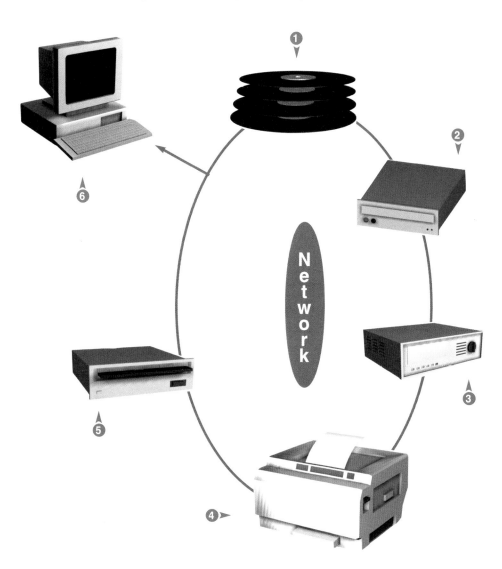

In a LAN, computers that share with others resources which belong to or are physically connected to them are called 'servers'. Computers that use the resources of other computers are called 'clients' (or 'client stations' or simply 'stations').

1 Hard disks.

2 CD-ROM.

3 Fax/Modem.

4 Printer.

5 Optical disk.

6 Client station.

When, in a LAN, no PC functions as a dedicated server (i.e. when each PC can be both server and client), the network is known as a 'peer-to-peer network'. This is the case with the Windows 95/98 network.

This is an example of a peer-to-peer LAN in which each PC can use its own hard disks and printers as well as those of any other PC.

1 PC.

2 Printer.

3 PC port connection.

Using the hard disks of other PCs means gaining access to them through the network as if they were installed on your own computer. Though it might sound obvious, you can use these disks only if the other computers are switched on and running Windows. This problem inevitably arises in a 'peer-to-peer' network in Windows for Workgroups, Windows 95, Windows 98 or Windows NT Workstation. Other networks that use a dedicated server do not have this problem as each PC communicates only with the server, which is normally always on. Bear in mind that you could experience difficulties accessing computers through the network if their owner is away, if the office is closed or if the PCs are out of order.

Sharing resources in a peer-to-peer local area network

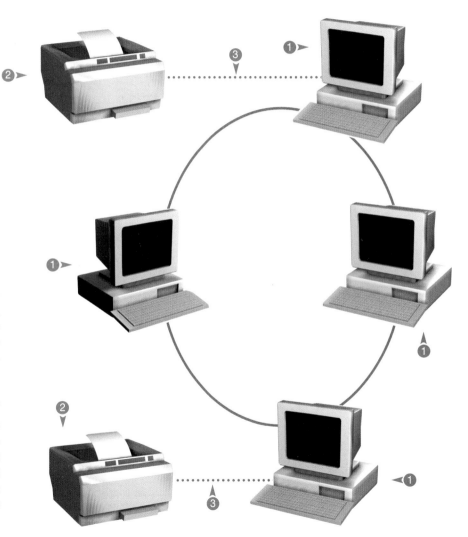

Sharing resources in a local area network with a dedicated server

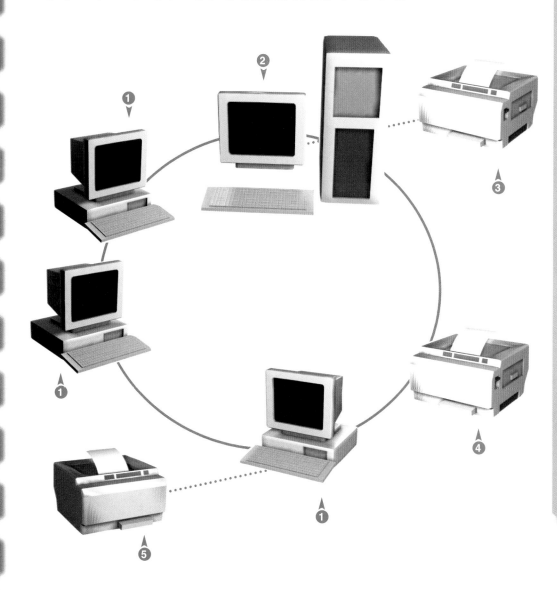

A LAN that includes one or more specialised server is more efficient than a peer-to-peer network. In such a network, the other machines are clients of the server. In some cases, clients can share their printers with others, but the sharing is then controlled by the server.

1. Client station.

2. *Dedicated* server.

3. Printer connected to the parallel port of the server.

4. Network printer with an internal network adapter.

5. Local printer connected to the parallel port of the PC.

LAN interconnection hardware

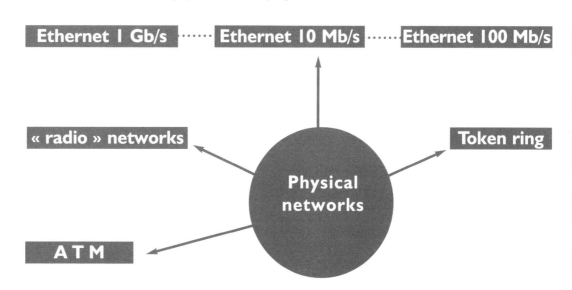

Here is a list of hardware you would need to run your LAN:

1. Network adapter. This is generally a card in the PC.

2. 'Client' and 'server' network software and the driver for the card.

3. Specific, intermachine network cables.

Different types of 'physical' local area networks

Technicians distinguish two independent components in LANs. The 'physical' component (known as the 'physical' network) is concerned with an electrical connection and signals that enable machines to recognise each other and co-operate. The 'logical' part (known as the 'logical' network) is concerned with the type of software that organises the sharing of resources, security, etc.

Ethernet 1 Gb/s ⋯⋯ **Ethernet 10 Mb/s** ⋯⋯ **Ethernet 100 Mb/s**

« radio » networks

Token ring

Physical networks

ATM

The Ethernet

Data transmission and collisions

The 'Ethernet' (no connection with the Internet) is currently the most widespread 'physical' network and thus the only one that will be discussed in this book. It features a theoretical bandwidth of 10 Mb/s. In practice, however, its actual rate is far lower, as it must be shared by and between the various connected machines.

The Ethernet functions as follows. Each machine that wants to send data through the network can do so after having 'looked' on the network to check that there is no data already in the queue (just like a pedestrian who wishes to cross the street). The data sent leaves simultaneously for all the machines, but only those machines for which it is intended intercept and process it. At times, data collisions occur (as on the road): either because the data leaves at the same time from two electrically equidistant machines, or because it leaves at different moments but arrives at the same place on a cable because of different cable lengths to cover. Fortunately, such collisions cause no physical damage to the network. Ethernet solves the problem automatically by annulling the data and asking the two machines involved to send their data again. Each machine waits a random amount of time, so that collisions will not reoccur.

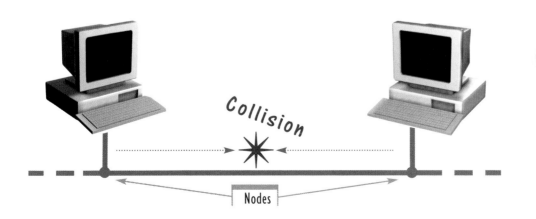

Collision

Nodes

There are two main ways of connecting machines in an Ethernet type of network: by 'bus' or by 'star' interconnection. We are going to see these two types of interconnection in the following pages.

'Bus' cabling: theory...

The machines are linked in parallel.

This is the simplest and most economical topology, but also the least flexible and least secure. If a problem occurs with the cable or if an adapter fails, the entire network is subsequently blocked.

● = node

...and practice

In this type of cabling, the following are most often used:

1. 50-ohm coaxial cable with BNC connector (quantity = number of machines minus one; 50 ohm is the resistance of the cable).

2. 50-ohm BNC tees (quantity = number of machines).

3. 50-ohm BNC 'plugs' or 'terminators' at each end of the network (quantity = two, regardless of the number of machines).

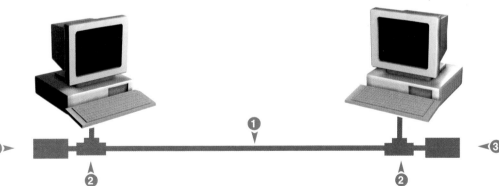

In order to use a bus topology you need network adapters (cards) with a 'BNC' connector, which is not found on all cards – and certainly not on 100 Mb/s Ethernet cards.

Hardware used in a bus local area network

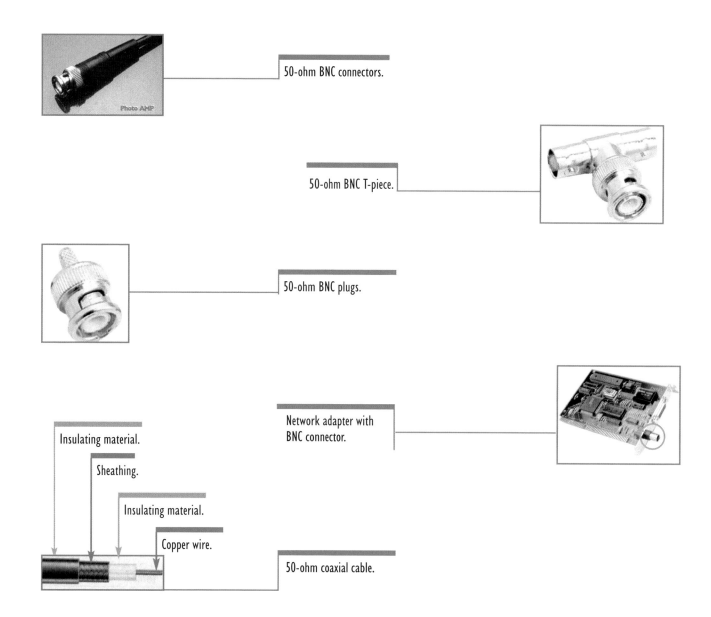

50-ohm BNC connectors.

50-ohm BNC T-piece.

50-ohm BNC plugs.

Network adapter with BNC connector.

Insulating material.

Sheathing.

Insulating material.

Copper wire.

50-ohm coaxial cable.

'Star' cabling: theory ...

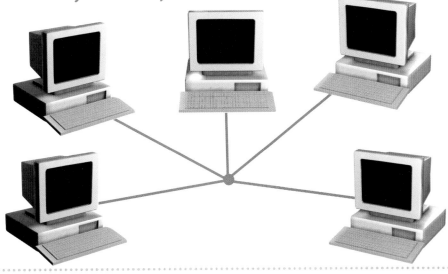

All the machines are connected to a common terminal.

.... **Note** ....

The advantage of the star topology is that each machine is independent. If one is disconnected, or its cable or network adapter fails, it will not cause the entire network to fail. Machines may, to a certain extent, be added or removed without affecting other users.

● = **node**

... and practice

Each machine is actually linked to a control box called the 'hub' through a flat, twisted-pair cable with an RJ45 connector at each end. The hub may be passive or may require a 230 V power supply connection.

1 The hub.

2 Twisted-pair cables, RJ45 connectors on either end.

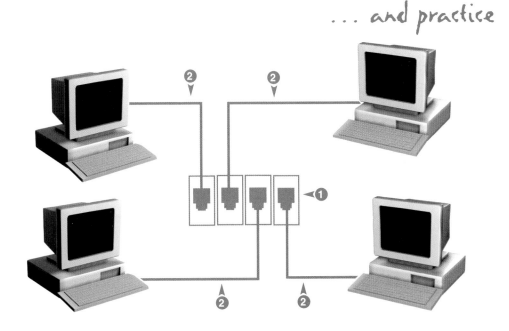

Hardware used in a star local area network

RJ45 connector.

A 12-slot hub.

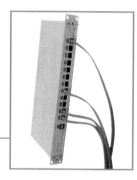

Interior of twisted cable used to connect the computers to the hub, with an RJ45 connector at each end.

Network adapters for connection with a hub.

Network protocols

The machines send and receive data over 'physical' networks such as the Ethernet, but they talk to each other using what is known as a network 'protocol' (the 'language' of the network). There are various network protocols. The most common on PCs running Windows 95 or 98 are **NetBEUI**, **IPX/SPX** (useful if you need to connect to a Novell NetWare server) and **TCP/IP** (which has been around for years thanks to the Internet and **UNIX** workstations, which use only this protocol). Apple Macintosh computers were designed to use the proprietary AppleTalk protocol, but can accept other protocols such as **TCP/IP.**

The interconnected machines (**PCs**, printers etc.) may use different protocols; however, only those that use a common protocol can communicate.

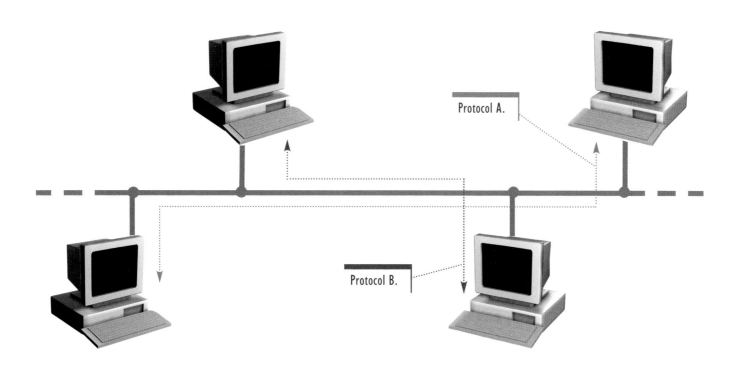

Protocol A.

Protocol B.

Resource-sharing services

The right protocol on the diskettes or **CD-ROM** of the selected operating system alone will not enable you to communicate with another machine. You must also have sharing ('server') and ('client') functions for the resources of the different machines connected to the network.

We have already mentioned these resources: they are the hard disks and the printers. With Windows 95, you can even fax from a single fax-modem if you install the Microsoft Fax feature. This was supplied as a standard feature with Windows 95, but was dropped from Windows 98. In both Windows 95 and 98, modems can also be shared through third-party software (non-standard feature).

Resource-sharing services in theory accompany the protocols, though this is not always the case. For example, the Windows **NT Workstation Pack** is delivered with the AppleTalk protocol but not with the 'service' that allows resource sharing with Macintosh computers. We can achieve this by purchasing specific software (such as **PC Mac LAN**).

LAN operating systems

When you have chosen your physical network (e.g. Ethernet 10 Mb/s or Ethernet 100 Mb/s), and your cabling topology from among those available for that network (bus link with coaxial cable and **BNC** connectors; star connection, with hub, twisted-pair cables and RJ45 connectors; optical fibre links; 'radio' links, etc.), you must also select your network operating system (**NOS**).

The **NOS** (also known as the 'Network Manager') is software that, depending on the case, is added to the operating system of the machine or combines both **NOS** and **OS** (operating system) functions. The server can control who can access which parts of the network and in this way can reduce the amount of traffic, or number of people using the network at the same time.

File- and print-sharing services (vary depending on the **NOS**)

Network protocol

OS + NOS or an NOS which combines both OS and NOS.

Network card+driver

PC

Each **NOS** has its own philosophy, its own network adapter, drivers, etc., and it is not always easy to migrate from one to another. **This often means having to** reconsider everything from scratch, even if some operating systems are supplied with migration tools.

Initially, many **NOS** were proprietary and therefore isolated systems. Today, most of them can work with other systems.

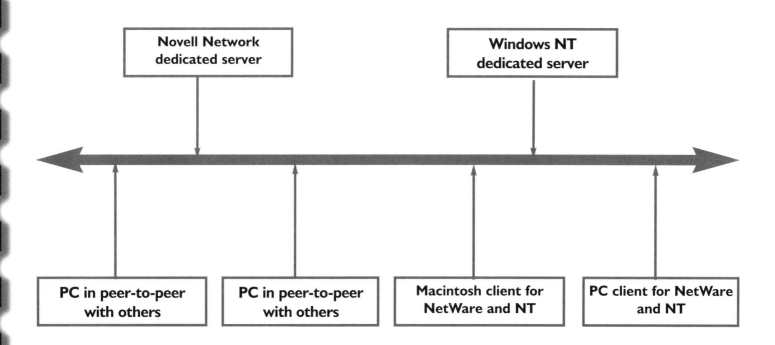

The most important Network Operating Systems

NetWare from Novell: both OS and NOS, this works only in dedicated–server mode, not in peer-to-peer mode. The user interface on the server is in character mode (except for NetWare 5 and newer versions) and proprietary, and thus an additional client machine (under Windows, for instance) is needed to administer the server, but the server can be run and the network administered from the console. NetWare servers accept most 'clients' (DOS, Windows NT, Windows 3.x/95/98, Mac, UNIX etc.). The server can run only specific applications called NLMs. For a long time, the basic protocol was IPX/SPX, and a new product had to be introduced so that it could run with TCP/IP (added to IPX/SPX, in fact). The most recent versions are native TCP/IP.

Windows NT Server: both OS and NOS, this is not designed to operate in 'peer-to-peer' mode. It accepts most clients. Its administration takes place directly on the server, which has the Windows 95/98 interface, and it accepts most applications written for Windows 95/98/NT, as well as some Windows 3.x applications. The main protocol used to be NetBEUI, but it is very easy to have it operate with TCP/IP only.

Windows for Workgroups: this used to be an add-on package for Windows 3.1x (it is no longer current). It provided peer-to-peer features when used with other machines under Windows for Workgroups. It could also be used as a 'client' of a Novell NetWare server.

Windows 95, 98 and NT: these include as standard all the elements required to operate in peer-to-peer mode, and can also be used as clients for Novell NetWare servers or Windows NT Servers. Today, even most UNIX servers are open to Windows 95, 98 and NT clients.

There used to be many add-on products for DOS or Windows (especially 3.x) that provided peer-to-peer network features. As Windows 95 has nearly everything necessary, most of the add-ons are now obsolete. It is nonetheless worth mentioning two of them: LANtastic from Artisoft, which provides a richer management under Windows 95, and PC MacLan, which enables Windows 95/98 and Windows NT Workstation to operate in peer-to-peer mode with Macintosh computers.

Resource mapping

If you have not already done so during installation, you must decide on the sharing of resources as well as the access rights of each user to these resources. Irrespective of the selected physical network, network protocol or **NOS**, it will often not be possible for other machines to use the shared resources if these resources are not mapped.

Mapping the hard disk 'C:' from a **PC** called 'Machine 1' consists of deciding to call it, for example, 'D:' on the network or on any other machine in the network that does not have a hard disk. It is not possible to have two 'C:' hard disks on the same machine. See the diagram on p. 31.

Resource mapping is essential with **DOS** and Windows 3.x; it is not always necessary (although it may be useful) with Windows 95/98/**NT** 4.x–5.x, as 32–bit applications (designed specially for these operating systems) are capable of browsing directly other machines' drives shared through the network.

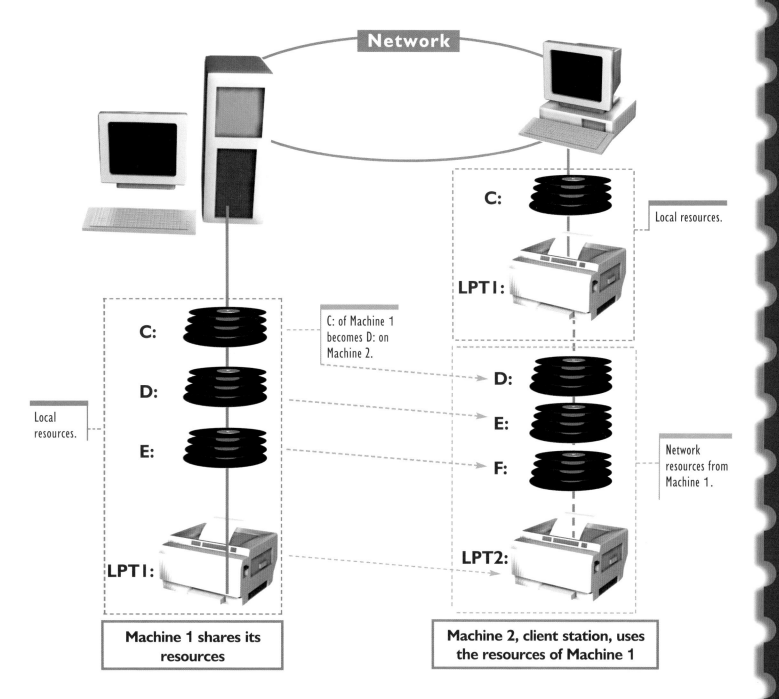

Network

C: of Machine 1 becomes D: on Machine 2.

Local resources.

Local resources.

Network resources from Machine 1.

Machine 1 shares its resources

Machine 2, client station, uses the resources of Machine 1

Chapter 2

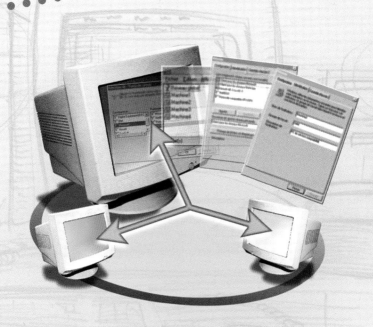

Installing the Windows 95/98 local area network

Pre-installation checklist

R unning Windows 95/98 in a network is not complicated. However, it will not be enough to install the necessary hardware (network adapter in each **PC** and inter-**PC** cables): you will also have to install a number of software functions and proceed to various settings. Normally, no network function is installed when you buy a computer under Windows 95/98, even if some (very few) machines have an internal network adapter (a card added in one of the bus connectors or hardware integrated in the motherboard). As you have already seen, in fact, there are many types of network software that can be used with a **PC** under Windows, and an appropriate network client is required each time. The network client in question here is that supplied with Windows 95/98 to facilitate two **PCs** operating in peer-to-peer mode. Before you do anything, you must check that no network hardware or software components have already been configured by Windows 95/98. It is possible that a prior installation has already been carried out by you, the manufacturer or the assembler of the **PC**. To check whether network components are already installed in your **PC**, click on the *System* icon and then the *Network* icon (both in the *Control Panel*): the first to check for hardware (network adapter), the second to check for software components (drivers, protocols, etc.).

HOW TO

To access the *System* icon, proceed as follows:

Either

1. Click *Start*, then *Settings*, *Control Panel* and then double-click the *System* icon;

Or

2. Double-click the *My computer* icon (on the *Desktop*), then *Control Panel*, and then the *System* icon.

TIP

You must first check that there is no network adapter physically installed in your PC. If there is one, remove it. Don't forget to turn the power off first. A few PCs include a network adapter on the motherboard. If this is the case with your machine you must disable the hardware (see your PC's manufacturer's manual).

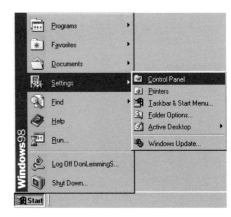

Check network hardware components

Start / Settings / Control panel / System icon

Double-click the System icon in the Control Panel.

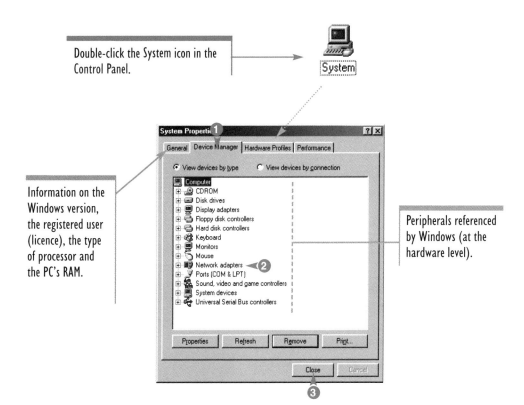

Information on the Windows version, the registered user (licence), the type of processor and the PC's RAM.

Peripherals referenced by Windows (at the hardware level).

Check first that there is no network adapter physically installed in the PC; you must disable it (see manufacturer's manual) if your PC includes a network adapter on the motherboard.

Checklist

Before you install your hardware and software, you must check whether there are any Windows 95/98 network components already installed.

1. Click the *Device Manager* Tab.

2. If there is no *Network adapters* heading go to step 3.

   If there is a *Network adapters* heading, go to step 1 on the next page.

3. Click the *Close* button to end the procedure, and go directly to the 'Check network software elements' section.

Checklist

1 Click the '+' sign to view any network adapters already installed by Windows 95/98.

2 Select (click) the existing network adapter (do not touch *Dial-Up Adapter* if the Internet is installed on your machine).

3 Click the *Remove* button.

Device manager with network adapter

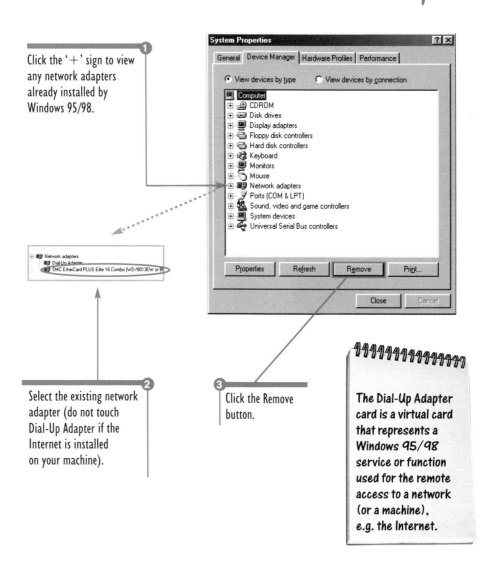

Click the '+' sign to view any network adapters already installed by Windows 95/98.

Select the existing network adapter (do not touch Dial-Up Adapter if the Internet is installed on your machine).

Click the Remove button.

The Dial-Up Adapter card is a virtual card that represents a Windows 95/98 service or function used for the remote access to a network (or a machine), e.g. the Internet.

Windows warns you that you are about to remove a device from your system.

Click the *OK* button.

Confirm device removal

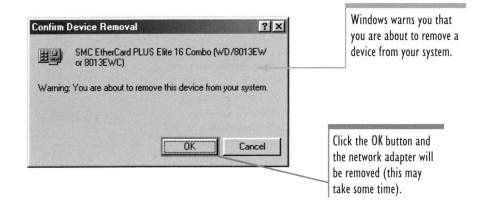

Windows warns you that you are about to remove a device from your system.

Click the OK button and the network adapter will be removed (this may take some time).

Restart the computer

Click the Yes button to finish.

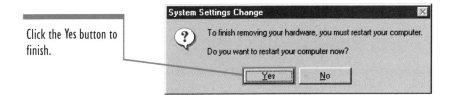

The changes made (removal of the network adapter) do not have immediate effect: they will be taken into account only when the computer is restarted.

Click the *OK* button.

When Windows has been restarted, go to the next step: 'Check network software components'.

Warning: When you remove a 'network adapter' in the list of devices recognised by Windows 95/98, you presume that the network adapter is physically absent from the PC. If it is not the case, the adapter may be automatically detected by Windows next time you start the PC. To avoid this, disable rather than remove the adapter.

Checklist

You are going to check whether there are any Windows 95/98 components already installed.

Double-click the *Network* icon in the *Control Panel*.

1 There must be nothing here, except *Dial-Up Adapter* and protocol lines if the Internet is already installed on the machine. If there is something else, then your PC is fitted with a network adapter integrated on the motherboard, or installed at some other time. In such a case, select all the visible lines, except those concerned with the *Dial-Up Adapter* card and click the *Remove* button. When the PC is restarted, these changes will have taken effect.

2 Click the *OK* button to finish.

Check network software components

Start / Settings / Control Panel / Network icon

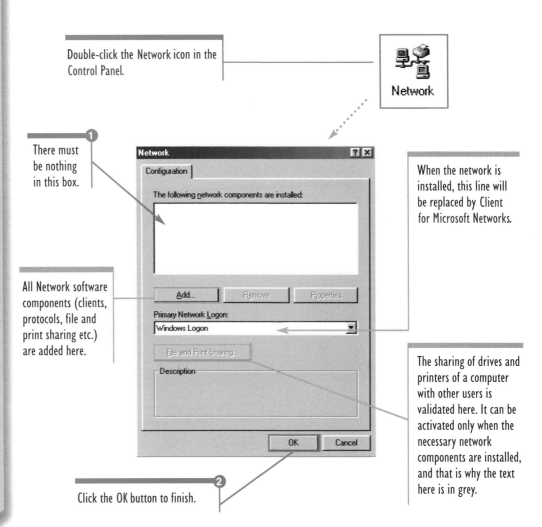

Double-click the Network icon in the Control Panel.

1 There must be nothing in this box.

All Network software components (clients, protocols, file and print sharing etc.) are added here.

When the network is installed, this line will be replaced by Client for Microsoft Networks.

The sharing of drives and printers of a computer with other users is validated here. It can be activated only when the necessary network components are installed, and that is why the text here is in grey.

2 Click the OK button to finish.

Installation procedures

The block diagram summarises the three possible installation procedures: automatic, semi-automatic and manual. These depend on whether or not your network adapter is properly recognised by Windows. Please note that for the installation of the network, your **PC** does not need to be connected to another machine. This connection can be made at a later stage when testing the connection.

NOTE

Some screen snapshots shown in this chapter may be different from those you will see when carrying out your own installation because they depend on the network adapter used.

The System icon in the Control Panel shows you which Input-Output (I/O) addresses and which interrupt requests (IRQs) are already used. It is difficult to recommend values, as these can vary from one machine to the other and from one network card to the other. What is certain is that IRQ 5 is available if you do not have an LPT2 physical parallel port.

Type of network adapter

↓

ISA (industry standard architecture) non–PNP (plug & play) card Configurable by micro-switches or jumpers

↓

Configure the adapter.

↓

Switch off the PC. Insert the card. Switch on the PC.

↓

Let Windows 95/98 start up.

↓

Go to the section: 'Manual network installation'

Type of network adapter	
ISA non–PNP card **Configurable through supplied DOS software**	**PNP/PCI (peripheral connection interface) card** **Self-configurable under Windows 95/98**
Switch off the PC. Insert the card. **Switch on the PC.**	**Switch off the PC. Insert the card.** **Switch on the PC.**
Start under DOS (press F8 during loading).	**Let Windows 95/98 start completely.**

Run and use the configuration software provided with the adapter.	**The card is not recognised: nothing happens.**	**The card is recognised automatically .**

Go to the section: 'Semi-automatic installation of network adapter'.

Go to the section: 'Automatic installation of network adapter'.

Automatic installation of network adapter

Automatic installation is the default installation. It starts as soon as Windows is loaded if the adapter (network or otherwise) just installed in the **PC** has a **PCI** connector; this also works if it has an **ISA** connector, provided that the card and the **PC BIOS** are Microsoft *Plug & Play* (PnP) compliant. All these cards are usually recognised as soon as Windows is started. If this is the case, you will have no hardware settings (**IRQ, I/O, DMA,** etc.) to carry out.

If your card (the network adapter) is not recognised automatically by Windows, you will have to proceed to a semi-automatic installation which entails a rather lengthy search in the machine and all the hard disks. If this still does not work, then you will have to proceed to a manual installation, which requires being able to tell Windows about all the hardware settings; this entails adjusting the internal hardware settings either with the special software delivered with the card or through jumpers or micro-switches (so take care to keep the instructions).

HOW TO

There is no particular step to take to access this installation, because when Windows 95/98 finishes loading it leads you automatically through the dialogue boxes presented in this section.

TIP
Switch off your PC and all its peripherals, and then insert your network adapter. If it has jumpers or micro-switches, do not close the casing of the microcomputer: you will probably need to modify the settings in order to change the hardware as it is rare for the default hardware configuration not to conflict with other cards.

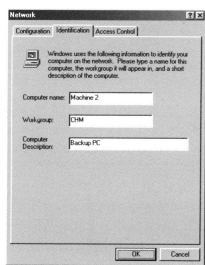

New device detected

It often happens that the device detected does not have the exact name of your card. The reason for this is that card manufacturers use various specialised chips which they do not always make themselves, and at times such a chip is detected by Windows. Nevertheless, for optimal card operation, it may be preferable to install – later on – the specific driver provided with the adapter.

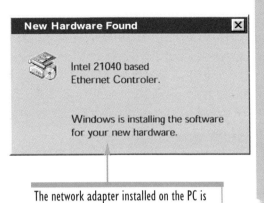

New Hardware Found

Intel 21040 based
Ethernet Controler.

Windows is installing the software
for your new hardware.

The network adapter installed on the PC is detected when Windows 95/98 is loading, once the PC has been switched on.

When Windows has finished loading, a window will tell you that a new device (network adapter) has been detected by displaying its references.

You do not need to do anything: you will reach the next step automatically.

Windows warns you that you must give a name to the computer so that it can be identified through the network.

Click OK to access the dialogue box where you can carry out this task.

Click the OK button.

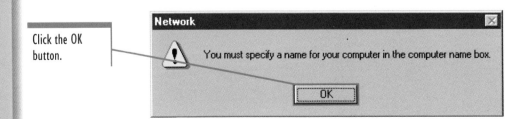

Network

You must specify a name for your computer in the computer name box.

OK

Network

Identification tab

This is where all the network software components (clients, protocols, file and print sharing etc.) can be viewed.

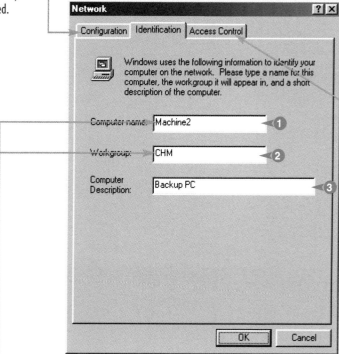

Here you can choose the type of access control that Windows will carry out on the users.

It is recommended, though not compulsory, that you do not exceed eight characters and that you avoid all special characters or spacing.

Checklist

1 Enter here the name you wish to give to the PC on the network. It is strongly recommended that you place this name on the casing of the computer itself (use a self-adhesive label).

2 You must also give the name of the workgroup to which you want the PC to belong. This can be the name of a person, a department or a company, for instance. PCs that do not belong to the same group will not be able to communicate with each other.

3 This description is not compulsory, but may be useful if the computers are in different rooms or offices.

Removing unnecessary components

Checklist

1 Click the *Configuration* tab.

2 Click the *IPX/SPX-compatible Protocol* line and then the *Remove* button to remove the *Client for NetWare Networks* and the *IPX/SPX-compatible Protocol*, which are unnecessary for what you are trying to do.

1 Click the Configuration tab.

This tab enables you to specify the computer name and the workgroup.

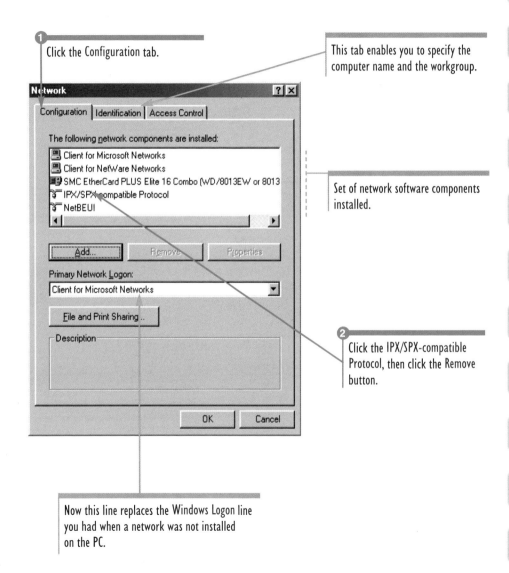

Set of network software components installed.

2 Click the IPX/SPX-compatible Protocol, then click the Remove button.

Now this line replaces the Windows Logon line you had when a network was not installed on the PC.

Checklist

The unneccesary components have been removed.

1 To begin configuring your machine click the *File and Print Sharing* button.

What remains is essential for the network to operate properly.

File and print sharing

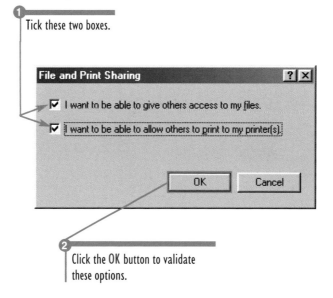

Tick these two boxes.

Click the OK button to validate these options.

Don't forget how to reach this dialogue box, as you will have to use it again to cancel the check-marks if you decide to remove sharing services.

Checklist

1 Tick these two boxes to enable the users of other PCs linked to the net-work to use the hard disks of this machine and the printer physically connected to its parallel port. Other dialogue boxes will enable you to define subsequently the conditions under which such sharing is to take place.

2 Click the *OK* button to confirm these options.

Configuration tab

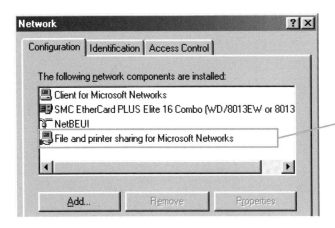

This line was added as a result of your ticking the preceding boxes. It corresponds to a Windows 95/98 service that uses resources: you must avoid this service on slower PCs with little memory, as these can access the resources of other machines, but will no longer be able to share theirs.

Access Control tab

Checklist

1 Click the *Access Control* tab.

2 Click the *OK* button to continue.

Leave this box ticked by default. It corresponds to the simplest but least secure method. It is recommended for private users or in order to maintain compatibility with computers under Windows 3.x fitted with the network add-on called Windows forWorkgroups.

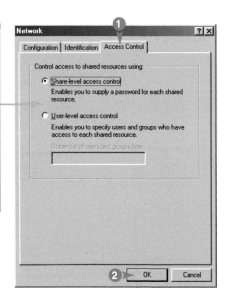

Access control at user level is the most secure, as only previously registered users can connect. It is more complicated to implement, however.

Network adapter resources

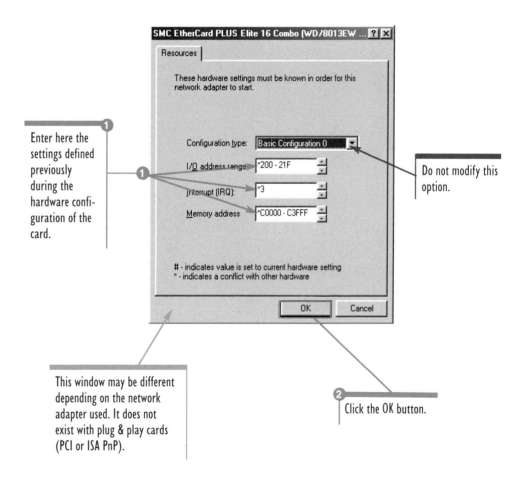

Enter here the settings defined previously during the hardware configuration of the card.

Do not modify this option.

This window may be different depending on the network adapter used. It does not exist with plug & play cards (PCI or ISA PnP).

Click the OK button.

Checklist

The system will search the Windows 95/98 CD-ROM for the files required for this network adapter to run properly.

① The files are copied from the Windows 95/98 CD-ROM on to the hard disk.

② Click this window every time it appears, to prevent failure of applications that require more recent files to run.

Copying files

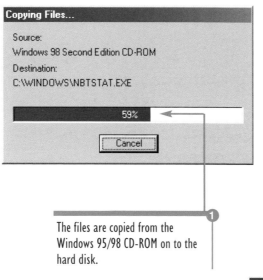

This type of message appears if you have updated certain Windows components since its installation. These new components are obviously not found on the original CD-ROM, so — unless instructed otherwise by a well-informed IT expert — you must avoid overwriting the new components with the old.

The files are copied from the Windows 95/98 CD-ROM on to the hard disk.

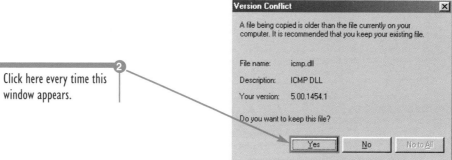

Click here every time this window appears.

You will obviously get an additional message if you forget to place the Windows 95/98 CD-ROM in its disk drive or if its path has changed since installation. In the latter eventuality, you will have to indicate the right drive and the correct folder (e.g. C:\WIN95 for Windows 95, C:\WIN98 for Windows 98).

Restart

Click the Yes button. The
computer will restart. This is
necessary for the changes
carried out to be taken
into account.

When the computer restarts, the Windows
logon starts with this dialogue box.

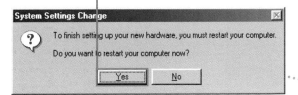

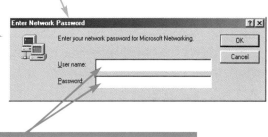

Select a User name and a Password; they will be
required to access the network subsequently.

You will note that, as you have configured the system, you cannot enter (connect to) the network
without the right user name and password. However, you can enter another user name and another
password to connect! In the most recent versions of Windows 95/98, i.e. those that include
Internet Explorer 4.x, it is possible to go much further in terms of security, in particular by authorising only users
who were listed previously.

Semi-automatic installation of network adapter
Start / Control Panel / Add New Hardware icon

Normally, if you have a recent network adapter and **PC**, what follows does not concern you, because the full automatic installation should have functioned properly. But if, by any chance, your system is not as modern (non-**PCI** or non-plug & play **ISA** cards, non-plug & play **BIOS**), or if a problem prevents Windows from automatically detecting the new network adapter that you have inserted in your **PC**, this procedure will not work. You have powered on again and waited for Windows to load completely and nothing happens in spite of the card (no dialogue box notifies you that Windows has recognised your card). You are therefore going to try the semi- automatic installation. This procedure consists of searching for all elements on the hard disk and in the computer that enable Windows to complete the information it had upon start-up. This operation may take several minutes and, in certain cases, the **PC** may stop responding. In many cases, it succeeds but if it still does not work, you can proceed to manual installation, which requires being able to tell Windows about all the hardware settings. This entails adjusting these internal hardware settings and those you will indicate to Windows, either with the special software delivered with the card (which you must not lose), or through jumpers or micro-switches (so take care to keep the instructions).

TIP

The first thing to do is switch off your PC and all its peripherals, and then insert your network adapter. If it has jumpers or micro-switches, do not close the casing of the PC because you will probably need to modify their settings in order to change the hardware configuration; for the one defined by default only rarely does not conflict with other cards.

HOW TO

There are two ways to access the *Add New Hardware* icon:

Either

1. Click *Start*, then *Settings*, *Control Panel*, and then double-click the *Add New Hardware* icon;

Or

2. Double-click *My Computer* in the *Desktop*, then on *Control Panel* and then on the *Add New Hardware* icon.

Add New Hardware Wizard dialogue box

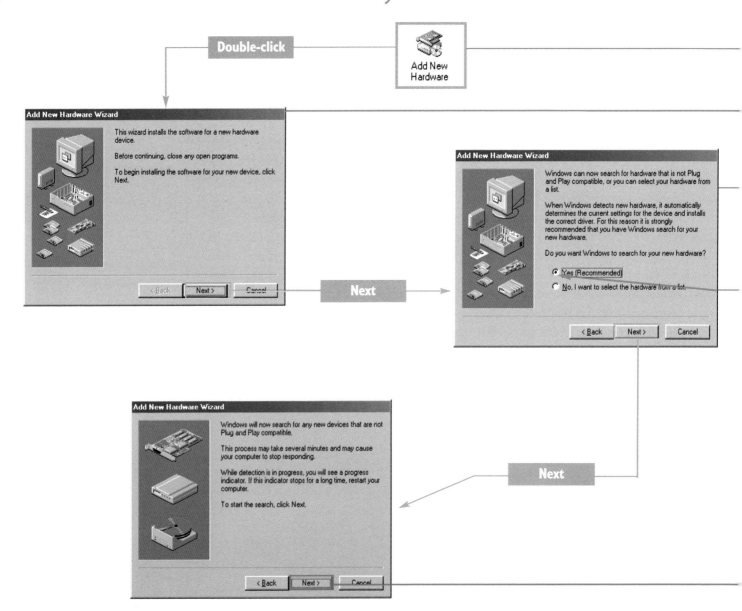

Double-click

Add New Hardware

Add New Hardware Wizard

This wizard installs the software for a new hardware device.

Before continuing, close any open programs.

To begin installing the software for your new device, click Next.

< Back   Next >   Cancel

Next

Add New Hardware Wizard

Windows can now search for hardware that is not Plug and Play compatible, or you can select your hardware from a list.

When Windows detects new hardware, it automatically determines the current settings for the device and installs the correct driver. For this reason it is strongly recommended that you have Windows search for your new hardware.

Do you want Windows to search for your new hardware?

○ Yes (Recommended)

○ No, I want to select the hardware from a list.

< Back   Next >   Cancel

Add New Hardware Wizard

Windows will now search for any new devices that are not Plug and Play compatible.

This process may take several minutes and may cause your computer to stop responding.

While detection is in progress, you will see a progress indicator. If this indicator stops for a long time, restart your computer.

To start the search, click Next.

< Back   Next >   Cancel

Next

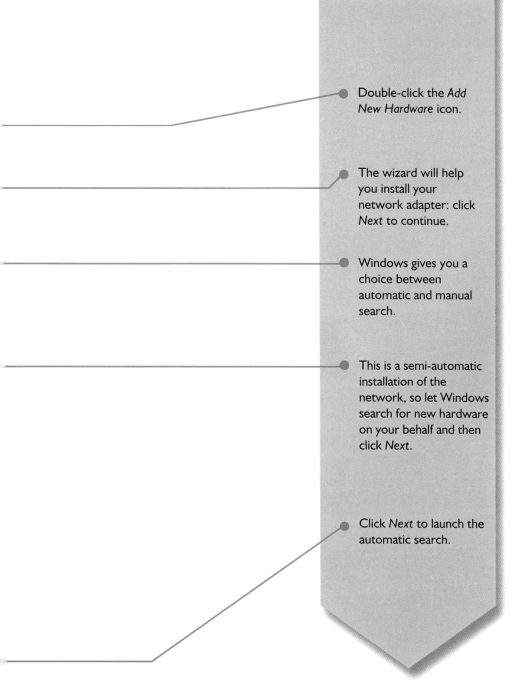

Double-click the *Add New Hardware* icon.

The wizard will help you install your network adapter: click *Next* to continue.

Windows gives you a choice between automatic and manual search.

This is a semi-automatic installation of the network, so let Windows search for new hardware on your behalf and then click *Next*.

Click *Next* to launch the automatic search.

Checklist

You are going to run the **Add New Hardware Wizard. This Wizard will try to recognise your network adapter or any other new device installed recently in the PC. As this is a semi-automatic installation, you will run an automatic search for the new network adapter installed in the PC.**

New hardware detection

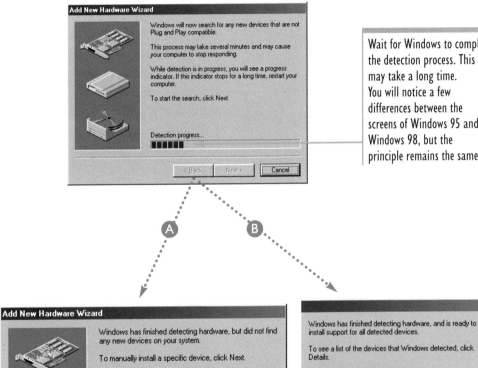

Wait for Windows to complete the detection process. This may take a long time. You will notice a few differences between the screens of Windows 95 and Windows 98, but the principle remains the same.

Windows 95/98 did not find any new devices.

Windows 95/98 has found the device.

The *Add New Hardware* wizard will now try to detect the network adapter. Wait for Windows to complete this detection process. Two possibilities may ensue:

A Windows 95/98 did not find the device;

Or

B Windows 95/98 detected the device.

Device not found

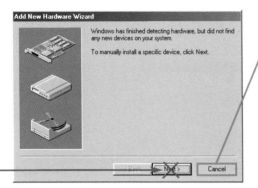

Add New Hardware Wizard

Windows has finished detecting hardware, but did not find any new devices on your system.

To manually install a specific device, click Next.

< Back | Next > | Cancel

Do not click Next!

Click the Cancel button and go directly to the 'Manual network installation' section.

A Windows 95/98 did not find the device. You will have to proceed to the manual installation.

Click *Cancel* and go directly to the 'Manual network installation' section.

Device found

B Windows 95/98 found the device but you must still make sure that the network adapter was detected properly.

Click the *Details* button to list the device or devices. This step does not exist in Windows 98 and the list is displayed directly in a slightly different dialogue box.

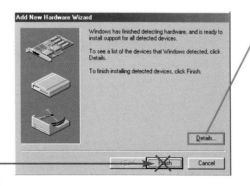

Add New Hardware Wizard

Windows has finished detecting hardware, and is ready to install support for all detected devices.

To see a list of the devices that Windows detected, click Details.

To finish installing detected devices, click Finish.

Details...

< Back | Finish | Cancel

Do not click Finish!

Click the Details button to list the device or devices. This step does not exist in Windows 98 and the list is displayed directly in a slightly different dialogue box.

Checklist

Windows now displays the name of the detected device. Normally, only the name of the network adapter should appear.

1. Click on the name of the card.

2. Click the *Finish* button to start the network adapter software installation.

Device detected

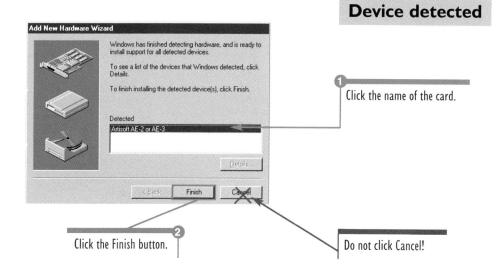

Click the name of the card.

Click the Finish button.

Do not click Cancel!

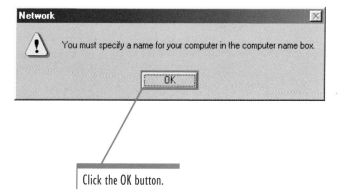

Click the OK button.

From here until the end of this section, the network installation procedure is similar to automatic installation.

Checklist

1. Enter here the name you wish to give to the PC on the network. It is strongly recommended that you place this name on the casing of the computer itself (use a self-adhesive label).

2. You must also give the name of the workgroup to which you want the PC to belong. This can be the name of a person, a department or a company, for instance. PCs that do not belong to the same group will not be able to communicate with each other.

3. This description is not compulsory, but may be useful if the computers are in different rooms or offices.

Network

Identification tab

This is where all the network software components (clients, protocols, file- and print-sharing, etc.) can be viewed.

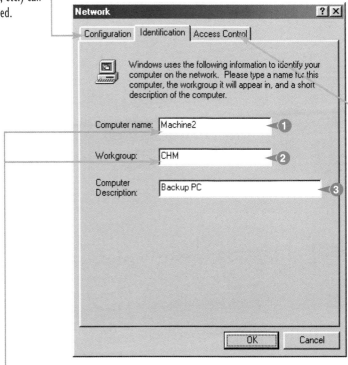

Here you can choose the type of access control that Windows will carry out on the users.

It is recommended that you do not exceed eight characters and avoid all special characters or spacing.

CHAPTER 2: INSTALLING THE LOCAL AREA NETWORK

57

Removing unnecessary components

Configuration tab

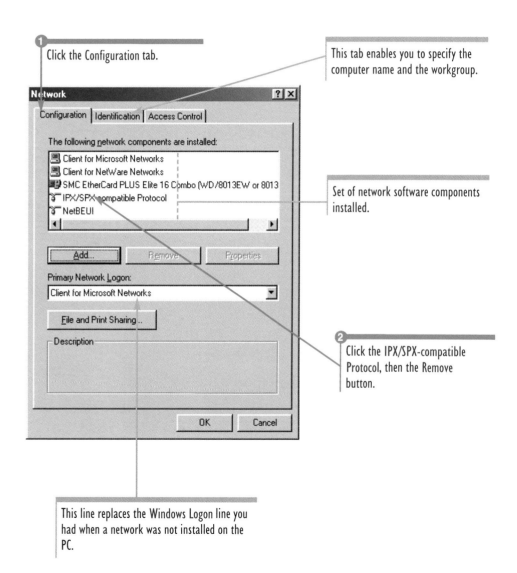

Click the Configuration tab.

This tab enables you to specify the computer name and the workgroup.

Set of network software components installed.

Click the IPX/SPX-compatible Protocol, then the Remove button.

This line replaces the Windows Logon line you had when a network was not installed on the PC.

① Click the Configuration tab.

② Click the *IPX/SPX-compatible Protocol* line and then the *Remove* button to remove the *Client for NetWare Networks* and the *IPX/SPX-compatible Protocol*, which are unnecessary in your case.

Configuration tab

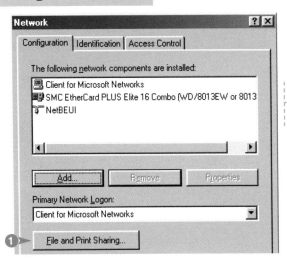

What remains in this window is essential for the network to operate properly.

Checklist

The unnecessary components have been removed.

1 Click the *File and Print Sharing* button.

File and print sharing

Checklist

1 Tick these two boxes to enable the users of other PCs linked to the network to use the hard disks of this machine and the printer connected to its parallel port. Other dialogue boxes will enable you to define subsequently the condition under which such sharing is to take place.

2 Click the *OK* button to validate these options.

1 Tick these two boxes.

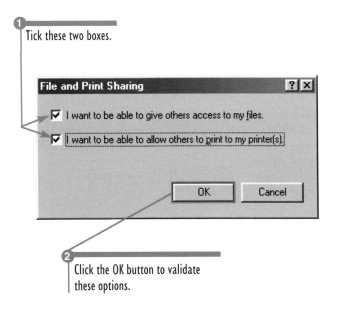

2 Click the OK button to validate these options.

Don't forget how to reach this dialogue box, as you will have to use it again to remove the check-marks if you decide to remove sharing services.

Configuration tab

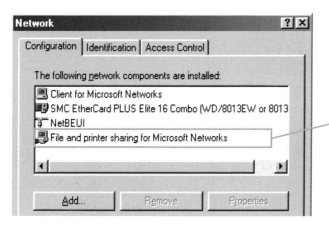

This line was added as a result of your ticking the preceding boxes. It corresponds to a Windows 95/98 service that uses resources; you must avoid this service on slower PCs with little memory, as they can access the resources of other machines, but will no longer be able to share theirs.

Access Control tab

Leave this box ticked by default. It corresponds to the simplest but least secure method. It is recommended for private users or if you need to maintain compatibility with computers under Windows 3.x fitted with the network add-on Windows for Workgroups.

Access control at user level is the most secure, as only previously registered users can connect. It is a little more complicated to implement, however.

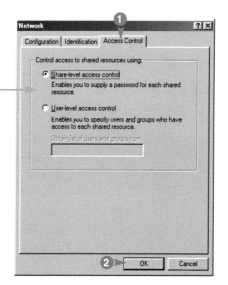

Checklist

1. Click the *Access Control* tab.

2. Click the *OK* button to continue.

Checklist

This window is used to enter the network adapter settings manually. It therefore does not appear with plug & play cards (PCI or ISA PnP).

1. Enter here the settings (which you should have written down) defined previously during the hardware configuration of the card (jumpers, micro-switches or software supplied).
2. Click the *OK* button.

Network adapter resources

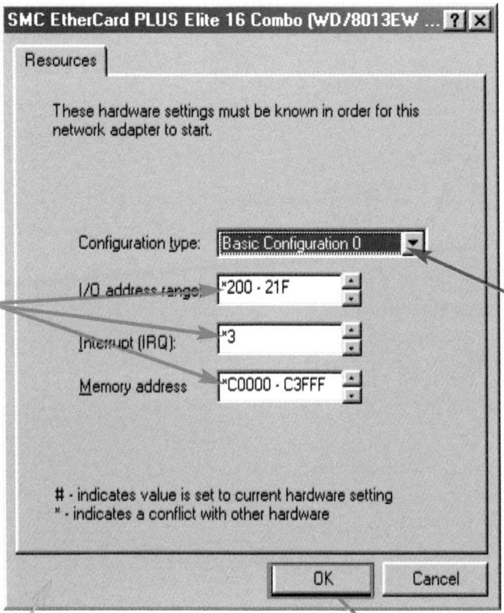

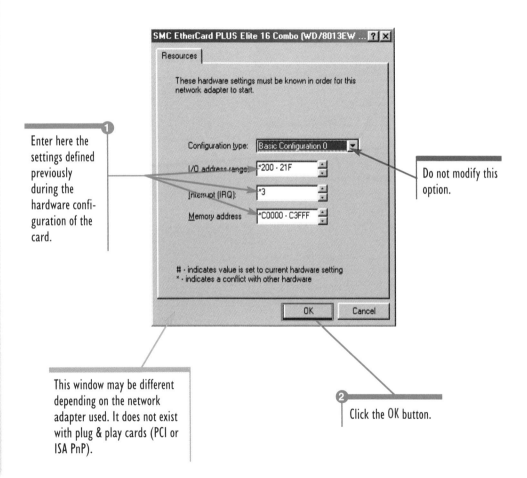

1 Enter here the settings defined previously during the hardware configuration of the card.

Do not modify this option.

This window may be different depending on the network adapter used. It does not exist with plug & play cards (PCI or ISA PnP).

2 Click the OK button.

Copying files

The system will search on the Windows 95/98 CD-ROM for the files required for this network adapter to run properly.

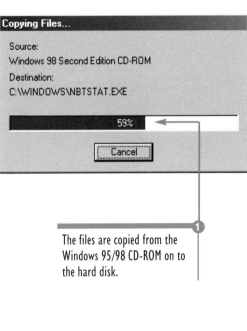

This type of message appears if you have updated certain Windows components since its installation. These new components are obviously not found on the original CD-ROM, so — unless instructed otherwise by a well-informed IT expert — you must avoid overwriting the new components by the old.

The files are copied from the Windows 95/98 CD-ROM on to the hard disk.

Click here every time this window appears.

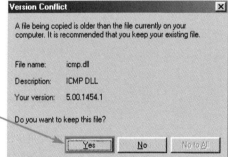

1 The files are copied from the Windows 95/98 CD-ROM on to the hard disk.

2 Click this window every time it appears, to prevent failure of applications that require more recent files to run.

You will obviously get an additional message if you forget to place the Windows 95/98 CD-ROM in its disk drive or if its path has changed since installation. In the latter eventuality, you will have to indicate the right drive and the correct folder (e.g. C\WIN95 for Windows 95, C\WIN98 for Windows 98).

Restart

Click the Yes button. The computer will restart. This is necessary for the changes carried out to be taken into account.

When the computer restarts, the Windows logon starts with this dialogue box.

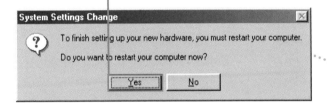

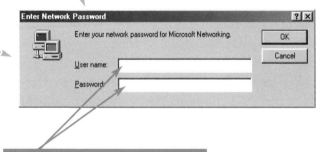

Select a User name and a Password; they will be required to access the network subsequently.

You will note that, as you have configured the system, you cannot enter in (connect to) the network without the right user name and password. However, you can enter another user name and another password to connect! In the most recent versions of Windows 95/98, i.e. those that include Internet Explorer 4.x, it is possible to go much further in terms of security, in particular by authorising only users who were listed previously.

Manual installation of network adapter
Start / Settings / Control Panel / Add New Hardware icon

The following will concern you only if you have not succeeded in installing the network adapter automatically or semi-automatically. The manual installation is necessary if you have an old system: if you have a **PC** that has no **PCI** connectors, **BIOS** that does not support the standard Microsoft plug & play for **ISA** connector cards or if your card is not plug & play, you will have to use this method. However, even when all these conditions seem to be met for an automatic or semi-automatic installation, various problems can prevent Windows from detecting the new network adapter (this applies also to all additional cards). Then you have no alternative but to proceed manually, which requires being able to tell Windows about all the hardware settings as with old **PCs**. This in turn entails adjusting these internal hardware settings and those you will indicate to Windows, either with the special software delivered with the card (which you must not lose), or through jumpers or micro-switches (so take care to keep the instructions). As we will see, the manual installation is more time–consuming than the other methods.

TIP

The first thing to do is switch off your PC and all its peripherals, and then insert your network adapter. If it has jumpers or micro-switches, do not close the casing of the microcomputer because you will probably need to modify their settings in order to change the hardware configuration: very rarely does the default configuration not conflict with other cards.

HOW TO

There are two ways to access the *Add New Hardware icon*:

Either

1. Click *Start*, then *Settings*, *Control Panel*, and then double-click the *Add New Hardware* icon;

Or

2. Double-click *My Computer* on the Desktop, then *Control Panel*, and then the *Add New Hardware* icon.

Checklist

You have started the *Add New Hardware Wizard*.

As you are proceeding with the manual installation, you are going to prevent Windows from configuring the hard-ware on your behalf.

1. Click the *Next* button.

2. Click the *No* box. This window does not exist in Windows 98; in this case continue until you reach the option *No, I want to select the hard-ware from a list*.

3. Click the *Next* button to continue.

Add New Hardware Wizard

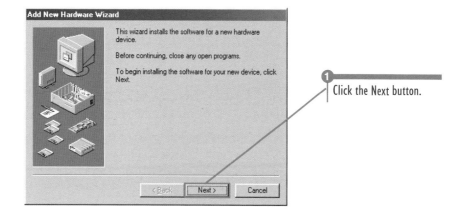

1. Click the Next button.

Click the No box. This window does not exist in Windows 98; in this case continue until you reach the option No, I want to select the hardware from a list.

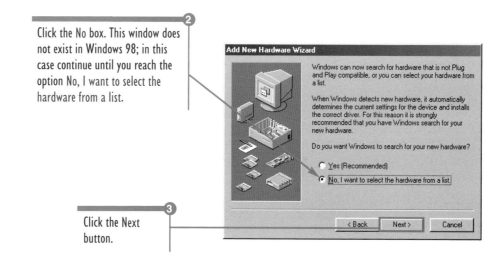

3. Click the Next button.

Checklist

You are going to select the type of hardware to install, i.e. a network adapter.

1. Click the *Network adapters* line.

2. Click the *Next* button.

Hardware types

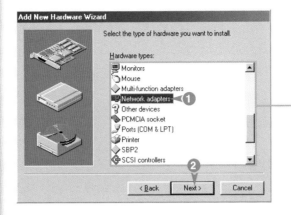

Windows displays the list of all hardware that can be installed on a PC.

The list of hardware shown here is arranged according to the Microsoft plug & play standard, in which each peripheral has ROM (read-only memory) containing codes that enable Windows (and the BIOS of the PC) to identify the category and reference of plug & play-compliant hardware. Here, everything will be done manually.

Select device

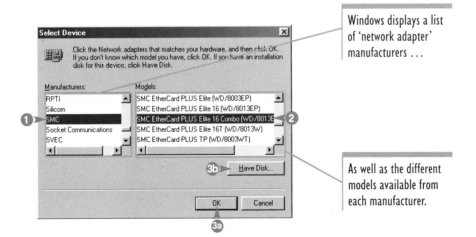

Windows displays a list of 'network adapter' manufacturers ...

As well as the different models available from each manufacturer.

Checklist

1. Click the name of the manufacturer of the network adapter installed in the PC.

2. Click the reference of the network adapter installed in the PC.

3a. Click the *OK* button if the adapter installed in the PC is visible in the list.

3b. Otherwise click the *Have Disk...* button.

Installing from a diskette

Checklist

① You must then insert the driver diskette delivered with the adapter and click the OK button. At times, however, the driver is installed by a non-standard and therefore different method: see the documentation delivered with the adapter and/or the driver.

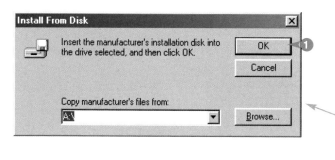

Install From Disk

Insert the manufacturer's installation disk into the drive selected, and then click OK.

OK ①
Cancel

Copy manufacturer's files from:

A:\ ▼ Browse...

This window will be displayed only if you previously selected Have Disk...

Adapter settings

Windows 95/98 warns you that there is a problem, it will propose default values for the Input/Output (I/O) addresses and for the IRQ which have nothing to do with those you have used to set the adapter hardware before running the network installation procedure. This is not serious as you will be able to adjust it later on.

Add New Hardware Wizard

Windows can install your hardware, using the following settings.

Warning: Your hardware may not be set to use the resources listed. You can use Device Manager to adjust these settings before restarting your computer. Click start, point to Settings, click Control Panel, click System, and then click the Device Manager tab. To change your hardware settings, see the documentation that came with your hardware.

To continue installing the software needed by your hardware, click Next.

Resource type	Setting	
Input/Output Range	0220 - 023F	Print...
Interrupt Request	05	
Memory Range	000E8000 - 000EBFFF	

< Back   Next >   Cancel

Click Next to continue.

Input/Output (I/O) Range and Interrupt Request (IRQ) are used by the operating system (e.g. Windows 98) to communicate with peripherals. With Windows 98, several peripherals can share the same IRQ, but not simultaneously.

Network

Identification tab

This is where all the network software components (clients, protocols, file and print sharing, etc.) can be viewed.

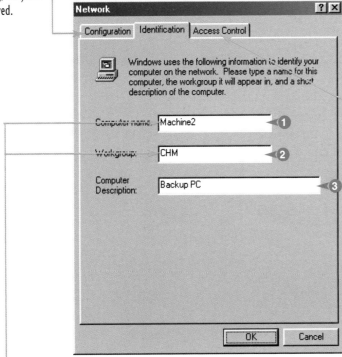

Here you can choose the type of access control that Windows will carry out on the users.

It is recommended, though not compulsory, that you do not exceed eight characters and that you avoid all special characters or spacing.

① Enter here the name you wish to give to the PC on the network. It is strongly recommended that you place this name on the casing of the computer itself (use a self-adhesive label).

② You must also give the name of the workgroup to which you want the PC to belong. This can be the name of a person, a department or a company, for instance. PCs that do not belong to the same group will not be able to communicate with each other.

③ This description is not compulsory, but may be useful if the computers are in different rooms or offices.

Checklist

1 Click the *Configuration* tab.

2 Click the *IPX/SPX-compatible Protocol* line and then on the *Remove* button to remove the *Client for NetWare networks* and the *IPX/SPX-compatible Protocol,* which are unnecessary in your case.

Removing unnecessary components

Configuration tab

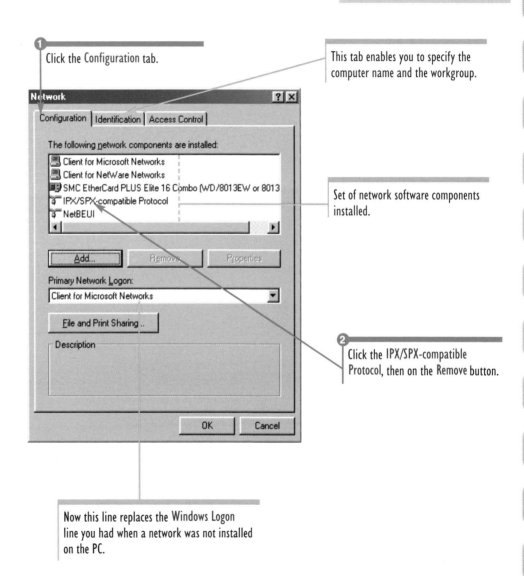

1 Click the Configuration tab.

This tab enables you to specify the computer name and the workgroup.

Set of network software components installed.

2 Click the IPX/SPX-compatible Protocol, then on the Remove button.

Now this line replaces the Windows Logon line you had when a network was not installed on the PC.

Checklist

The unnecessary components have been removed.

① Click the *File and Print Sharing* button to continue.

Configuration tab

What remains is essential for the network to operate properly.

File and print sharing

① Tick these two boxes.

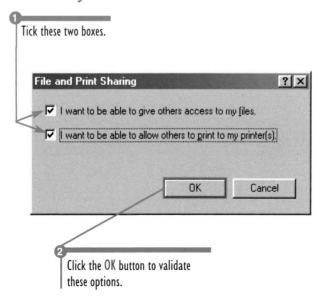

Don't forget how to reach this dialogue box, as you will have to use it again to remove the check-marks if you decide to remove sharing services.

② Click the OK button to validate these options.

Checklist

① Tick these two boxes to enable the users of other PCs linked to the network to use the hard disks of this machine and the printer physically connected to its parallel port. Other dialogue boxes will enable you to define subsequently the conditions under which such sharing will take place.

② Click the OK button to confirm these options.

Configuration tab

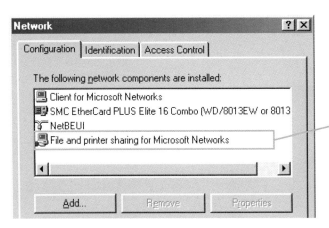

This line was added as a result of your ticking the preceding boxes. It corresponds to a Windows 95/98 service that uses resources; you must avoid this service on slower PCs with little memory, as these machines can access the resources of other machines, but will no longer be able to share theirs.

Access Control tab

Checklist

1. Click the *Access Control* tab.

2. Click the *OK* button to continue.

Leave this box ticked by default. It corresponds to the simplest but least secure method. It is recommended for private users or in order to maintain compatibility with computers under Windows 3.x fitted with the network add-on called 'Windows for Workgroups.'

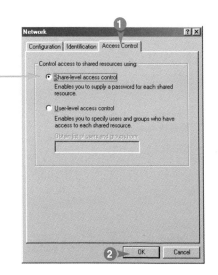

Access control at user level is the most secure, as only previously registered users can connect. It is a little more complicated to implement, however.

Copying files

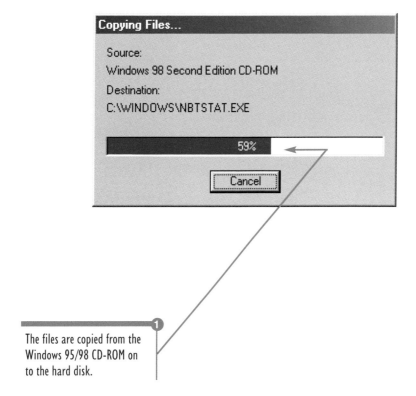

Copying Files...

Source:

Windows 98 Second Edition CD-ROM

Destination:

C:\WINDOWS\NBTSTAT.EXE

59%

Cancel

The files are copied from the Windows 95/98 CD-ROM on to the hard disk.

Checklist

The system will search the Windows 95/98 CD-ROM for the files required for this network adapter to run properly.

1 The files are copied from the Windows 95/98 CD-ROM on to the hard disk.

Checklist

Certain conflicts may appear when you are copying the files required for the network adapter to function properly.

1 Click this window every time it appears, to prevent failure of applications that require more recent files to run.

This type of message appears if you have updated certain Windows components since its installation. These new components are obviously not found on the original CD-ROM, so — unless instructed otherwise by a well-informed IT expert — you must avoid overwriting the new components with the old.

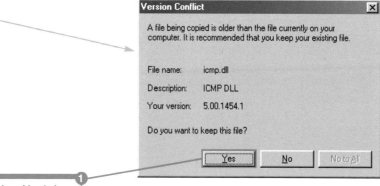

Version Conflict

A file being copied is older than the file currently on your computer. It is recommended that you keep your existing file.

File name: icmp.dll

Description: ICMP DLL

Your version: 5.00.1454.1

Do you want to keep this file?

[Yes] [No] [No to All]

Click here every time this window appears.

You will obviously get an additional message if you forget to place the Windows 95/98 CD-ROM in its disk drive or if its path has changed since installation. In the latter eventuality, you will have to indicate the right drive and the correct folder (e.g. C\WIN95 for Windows 95, C\WIN98 for Windows 98).

Finish installing software...

Windows has finished installing the software, i.e. the driver needed for the adapter to run properly.

Click the *Finish* button to continue.

Click the Finish button to continue.

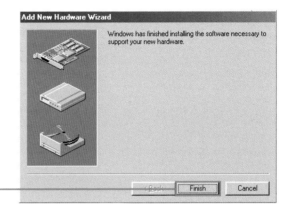

... and restart the computer

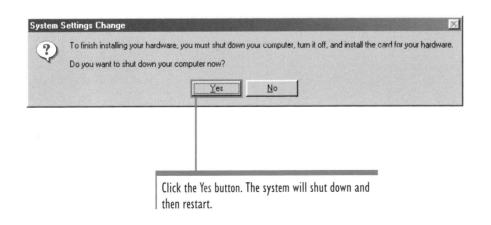

Click the Yes button. The system will shut down and then restart.

Click the *Yes* button. The system will shut down because Windows thinks that you are going to save the I/O and IRQ values it has proposed. It thinks you are going to change the hardware settings of the adapter accordingly (thus perhaps open the machine). In fact, you are going to save the hardware values of the adapter and change those of Windows further on.

Checklist

Windows will detect a configuration problem for the network adapter, and you will solve that problem in *System Properties*.

1. Click on *OK*.

2. Double-click on the *System* icon in the *Control Panel*; you will see an exclamation mark next to the network adapter installed; in your case, this means that the adapter is not set correctly. Double-click on that line (or click the *Properties* button).

System properties

Device Manager tab

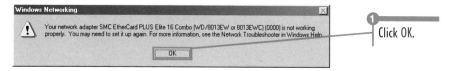

Click OK.

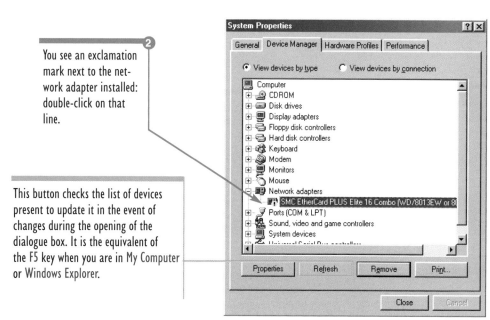

You see an exclamation mark next to the network adapter installed: double-click on that line.

This button checks the list of devices present to update it in the event of changes during the opening of the dialogue box. It is the equivalent of the F5 key when you are in My Computer or Windows Explorer.

During the software installation of a non-plug & play network adapter, Windows has no way of knowing the hardware settings. It therefore suggests default values that do not necessarily correspond to the choices you have made when you set your network adapter (before inserting it in the microcomputer, if the setting was carried out by means of jumpers; afterwards, if it was carried out with a special software delivered with the adapter). For the moment, the settings in the adapter and those in Windows do not correspond, hence the message. We will ask you to change this later to get everything back to normal.

Network adapter properties

General tab

The General tab reminds you that there is a problem with the adapter (Device status).

Click the Resources tab.

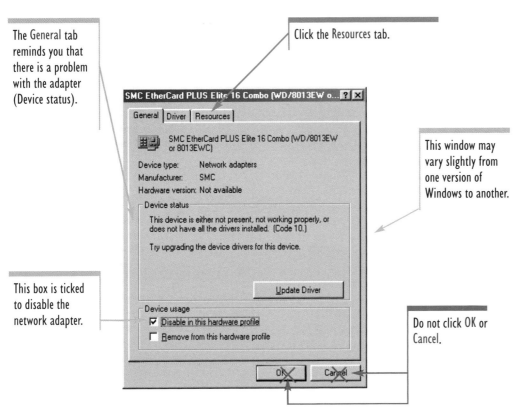

SMC EtherCard PLUS Elite 16 Combo (WD/8013EW o...

General | Driver | Resources

SMC EtherCard PLUS Elite 16 Combo (WD/8013EW or 8013EWC)

Device type: Network adapters
Manufacturer: SMC
Hardware version: Not available

Device status

This device is either not present, not working properly, or does not have all the drivers installed. (Code 10.)

Try upgrading the device drivers for this device.

Update Driver

Device usage
☑ Disable in this hardware profile
☐ Remove from this hardware profile

OK   Cancel

This box is ticked to disable the network adapter.

This window may vary slightly from one version of Windows to another.

Do not click OK or Cancel.

The *General* tab reminds you that there is a problem with the adapter, and you are going to solve it.

Click the *Resources* tab to find out about your network adapter.

This screen snapshot may differ depending on whether you are using the version of Windows 95 sold to the public (OS/R1), a version that was pre-installed in your computer under special agreement with Microsoft (OS/R2), or Windows 98.

Checklist

① The *Resources* tab shows those (I/O and IRQ) settings that are not physically selected on the adapter (hardware configuration).

② Select the *Interrupt Request* (IRQ) line.

③ Click the *Change Setting* button.

Resources tab

Information on the adapter: enabled or disabled, device status, references, etc.

The Resources tab shows those (I/S and IRQ) settings that are not physically selected on the adapter (hardware configuration).

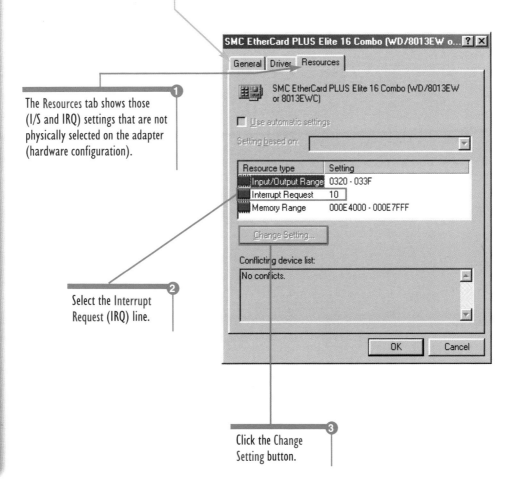

Select the Interrupt Request (IRQ) line.

Click the Change Setting button.

Resources tab

The system warns you of any conflicts between the network adapter and another device. Enter the correct value for the interrupt request (IRQ), and then check to make sure that no conflict persists.

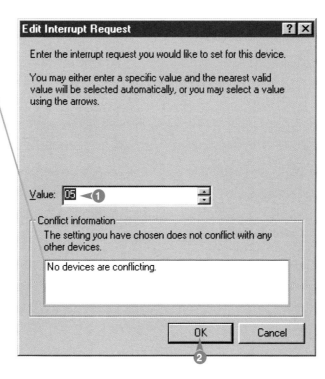

Checklist

1. Instead of 10, enter the value of the adapter hardware setting you had noted previously on paper ('05' in the example).

2. Click OK to continue.

Checklist

The dialogue box displays the resources and you see that the IRQ has changed. You must now change the Input/Output range.

1 Select the *Input/Output Range* line.

2 Click the *Change Setting...* button.

Select the Input/Output Range line.

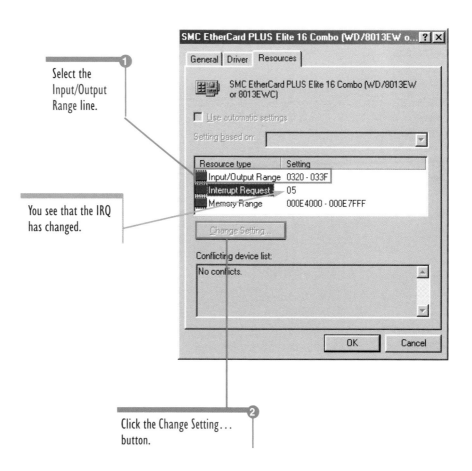

You see that the IRQ has changed.

Click the Change Setting... button.

Resources tab

The system warns you if there is any conflict between the network adapter and another device. Enter the correct value for the Input/Output Range, and then check to make sure that there is no conflict.

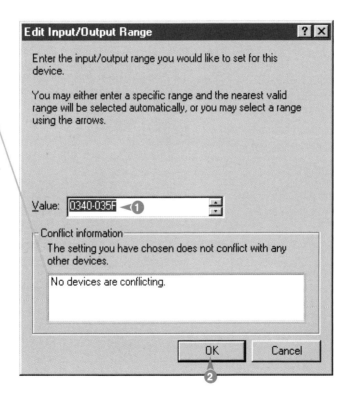

① Change the default setting and replace it with that used for the adapter hardware setting.

② Click OK.

Checklist

You now note that both settings are those defined for the adapter hardware (Interrupt Request and Input/ Output Range).

① Click *OK*.

You see that the Interrupt Request and the Input/Output Range have changed.

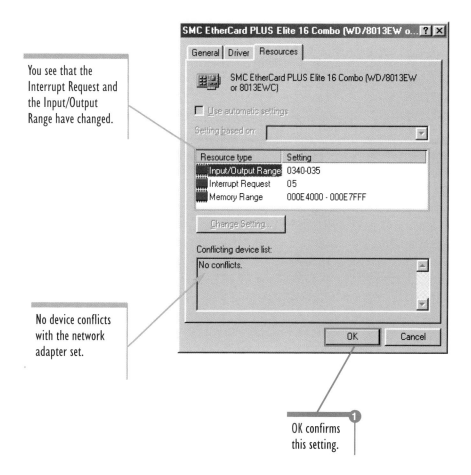

No device conflicts with the network adapter set.

① OK confirms this setting.

Restart

Windows informs you with a
slightly alarming message that you
have carried out major changes to
the system.

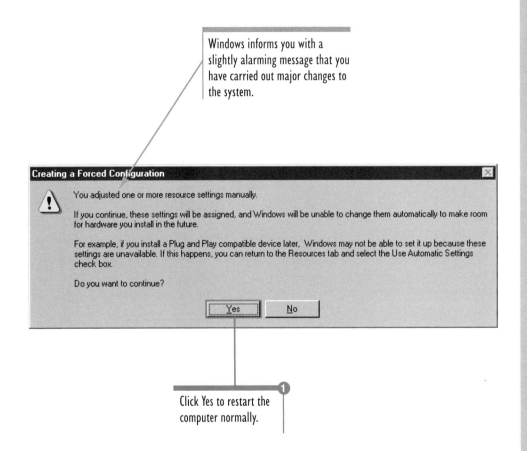

Creating a Forced Configuration

You adjusted one or more resource settings manually.

If you continue, these settings will be assigned, and Windows will be unable to change them automatically to make room
for hardware you install in the future.

For example, if you install a Plug and Play compatible device later, Windows may not be able to set it up because these
settings are unavailable. If this happens, you can return to the Resources tab and select the Use Automatic Settings
check box.

Do you want to continue?

Yes   No

Click Yes to restart the
computer normally.

Checklist

You have changed the
settings of your
network adapter. You
must now restart the
computer for the new
resources to be taken
into account.

Click Yes.

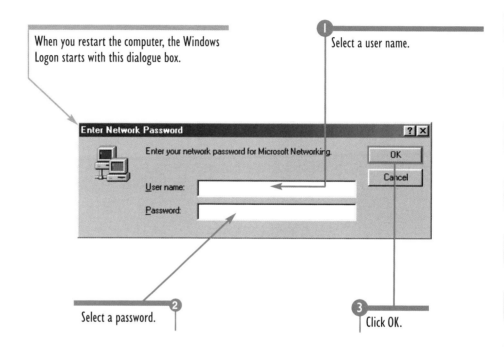

Checklist

To access the network, you must choose a user name and a password.

1. Select a user name.

2. Select a password. Write this down somewhere in case you forget it.

3. Click *OK*.

Enter Network Password

When you restart the computer, the Windows Logon starts with this dialogue box.

1. Select a user name.

Enter Network Password

Enter your network password for Microsoft Networking.

User name:

Password:

OK

Cancel

2. Select a password.

3. Click OK.

You will note that, as you have configured the system, you cannot enter (connect to) the network without the appropriate user name and password. However, you can enter another user name and another password. In the most recent versions of Windows 95/98, i.e. those that include Internet Explorer 4.x, you can go much further in terms of security, in particular by accepting only users who were listed previously.

Post-installation checklist
Start / Settings / Control Panel / System icon

After completing the installation of a network adapter, regardless of whether you installed it automatically, semi-automatically or manually, you should spend a few minutes checking that the hardware and software settings of your network have been entered correctly. You must check that your network adapter is recognised by Windows and is working properly. You must also check that the interrupt request (**IRQ**) and input/output range you have selected are saved properly and do not conflict with other devices. You will also notice a new icon on the Desktop called *Network Neighborhood*. This icon will enable you to browse from one **PC** to the other, provided you have set the parameters enabling you to do so.

HOW TO

There are two ways to access the *System* icon:
Either

1. Click *Start*, then *Settings*, *Control Panel* and then double-click the *System* icon;

Or

2. Double-click *My Computer* (on the Desktop), then *Control Panel*, and then *System*.

To access the *Network Neighborhood* icon, just go to the Desktop.

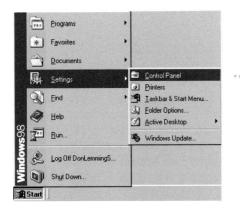

Checklist

1 Double-click the *System* icon.

2 Click the *Device Manager* tab.

3 Click the '+' sign to display the network adapters installed by Windows 95.

4 Double-click the name of the network adapter installed.

System properties

Device manager tab

Tab used to create and select various profiles depending on the devices connected at a particular moment (very useful for a portable with a docking station).

Double-click the System icon.

Click the Device Manager tab.

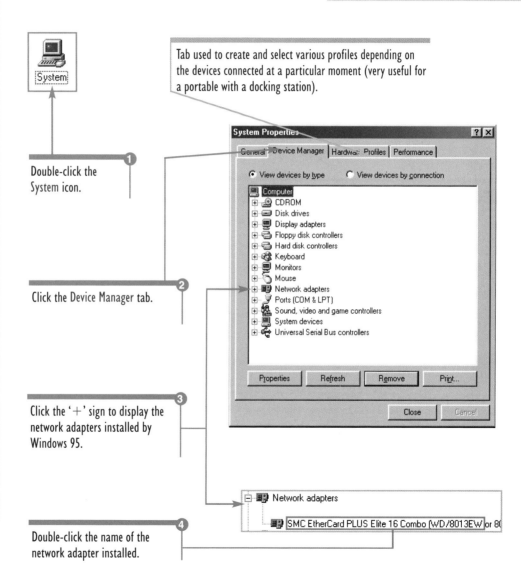

Click the '+' sign to display the network adapters installed by Windows 95.

Double-click the name of the network adapter installed.

Network adapter properties

General tab

You see a window giving you the properties of your network adapter.

This tab shows the Windows settings for this adapter (interrupt request (IRQ), input/output range, any memory range etc.). It also shows any conflicting cards.

Check to see if the device confirms that: *This device is working properly.*

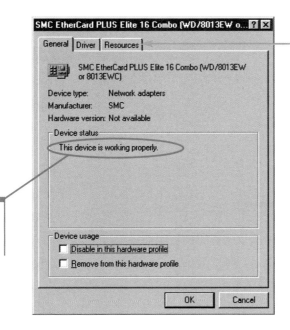

The General tab tells you the device status.

This screen snapshot may differ depending on whether you are using the version of Windows 95 sold to the public (OS/R1), a version that was pre-installed in your computer under special agreement with Microsoft (OS/R2) or Windows 98.

Checklist

1. Click the *Resources* tab.

2. You will find here the hardware settings of the adapter (in this case, an automatic plug & play adapter).

3. Check to make sure that the Conflicting device list confirms: *No conflicts*.

4. Click *OK* to finish the operation.

Network adapter properties

Resources tab

This tab provides information on the adapter: enabled or disabled, device status, references etc.

① Click the Resources tab.

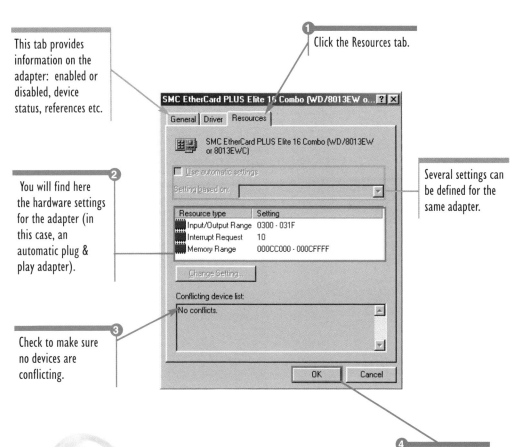

Several settings can be defined for the same adapter.

② You will find here the hardware settings for the adapter (in this case, an automatic plug & play adapter).

③ Check to make sure no devices are conflicting.

④ Click OK to end the procedure.

If the settings conflict with another card, network adapter or otherwise (because there may be several network adapters installed in a single PC), Windows will provide you with details to help you solve the problem.

Network Neighborhood

You will discover a new icon on the Desktop that will enable you to view other devices on the local area network.

My computer is a simplified Explorer. It gives access to disk drives, fixed and removable disks as well as to the Control Panel and the Remote Network Access icons (Internet).

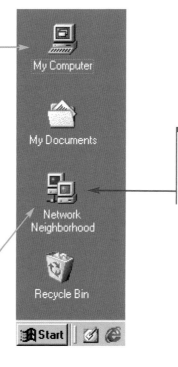

Double-click this icon only if the PC connection is in place.

Icon used to view other devices on the local area network.

The Network icon is new only if you installed the Windows 95 'Network' functions for the first time.

Chapter 3

TCP/IP

TCP / IP

Some users, especially within companies, may wish to use only TCP/IP, which is more efficient both for a **LAN** and a **WAN**, and which is *the* Internet and intranet protocol. When you install a network adapter and network functions on a **PC** under Windows 95, the TCP/IP protocol is not installed automatically. Windows 98, on the other hand, installs **TCP/IP** as soon as a network adapter is detected or declared by the user, but in such a way that the network functions are not immediately operational. You must therefore know how to install and how to configure **TCP/IP** if you want to use it. The default protocol for Windows 95 (and for Windows for Workgroups, the forerunner of Windows 95), which you learned to install in Chapter 2, is easy to install because it requires no particular settings (although sometimes settings can be changed to optimise it). **TCP/IP** cannot work without a minimum set-up and this is not always simple, even though the procedure has been simplified because it is used widely on the Internet. This chapter investigates how to replace the default local area network protocol (**NetBEUI**) by the **TCP/IP** protocol.

TIP

It might be prudent not to use TCP/IP at first. Make sure that the network is working properly and then switch to TCP/IP. This precaution may well save you unnecessary trouble.

HOW TO

There are two ways to access the *Network* icon:

Either

1. Click *Start*, then *Settings, Control Panel*, and then double-click the *Network* icon;

Or

2. Double-click *My Computer* (on the Desktop), then the *Control Panel* option and on the *Network* icon.

In theory ...

Both the Internet and **TCP/IP** grew out of the American military network, Arpanet, at the end of the 1960s. TCP/IP, which was developed in 1970 and was recognised as a standard in 1978, stands for 'transmission control protocol/Internet protocol'. The first modern computers to have integrated these protocols ran under **UNIX**. PCs took a little longer to start using them; it was the Internet explosion, in fact, that precipitated this boom. TCP/IP is made of two essential parts: **TCP** and **IP**. That is why we speak of a **TCP** network and an **IP** network. We will not go into technical details in this book, as others have done so already – and done it well. We shall instead limit the technical description to the minimum that is needed to find our way through the installation procedure.

With this protocol, each machine on the network – a **LAN** or the Internet world network – is identified through what is known as an **IP** address represented by four groups of a maximum of three digits, separated by a dot. These four groups give us 32 bits, i.e. theoretically about four billion addresses. This, however, is valid only if the **LAN** is not connected directly to the Internet (through a device called a router, using an **ISDN** line or a special permanent line leased at a very high cost from the local telecom operator). If your **TCP/IP** network is connected to the Internet, you will be limited to 254 addresses in the network of networks. The reason for this limit is that all addresses available on the Internet are divided into three classes in order to simplify its organisation and to define priorities. Class **A** and **B** addresses are reserved for very large organisations and universities. None of them are available any longer, as the network is virtually saturated. Since 1996, when a company requests a range of Internet addresses, it is assigned a Class **C** address, which has only 254 addresses. This may not be enough for a medium-sized or large company, and that is why subnetworks (subnets) have been invented, which operate as follows. Internally, the company uses a Class **A** network (16.7 million IP addresses) or Class **B** network (65 536 IP addresses)

Each group is composed of maximum three digits representing the numbers from 0 to 255 (i.e. 256 values). This is due to the fact that each group is composed of 8 bits, which gives 256 possibilities ($2^8 = 256$). 0 and 255 are reserved, so there are 254 values left.

and has organised them into subnets of 256 addresses, each being connected separately to the Internet through a router. The company-wide network finds its way through by applying a different subnet mask for each network, which filters the corresponding **IP** addresses. Understanding subnet masks requires some knowledge of the binary system on which information technology is built. For example, the mask 255.255.255.0 allows a subdivision into 256 subnets of 254 systems, each with a **Class B** address. Going into detail is quite complicated; our aim here is simply to give an idea of what a subnet mask is. Other solutions exist, such as building a conventional **Class A** or **B** network and linking it to the Internet through a gateway that will translate the addresses of the company's **LAN** into corresponding Internet addresses. None of this is within reach of the individual user or the small company, which, in any event, will be satisfied with a **LAN** of 254 computers.

Please note: the following description of the TCP/IP protocol installation is for a computer running Windows 95, running the peer-to-peer network of this operating system, with the NetBEUI protocol. If this is not the case of your PC, do not worry. The procedure adds TCP/IP but does not remove any other protocol. With Windows 98, there will be a few differences because the default protocol installed is TCP/IP instead of NetBEUI; but the basic principle remains the same. You can remove the other protocols if you are sure they are not essential. However, if your PC was already working in a network, or if you are not sure, do not remove the additional protocols: they will cause no problems other than to take up computer resources.

Installing TCP / IP

Start / Settings / Control Panel / Network icon

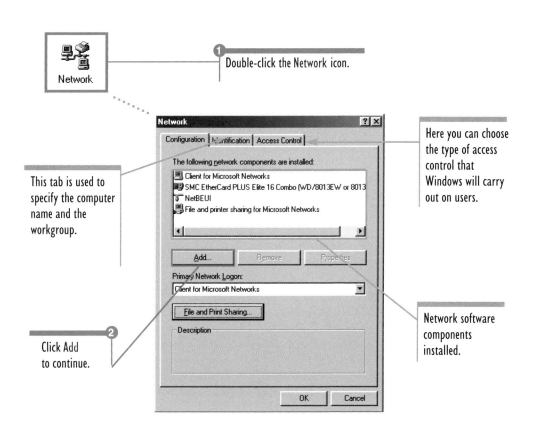

Double-click the Network icon.

This tab is used to specify the computer name and the workgroup.

Click Add to continue.

Here you can choose the type of access control that Windows will carry out on users.

Network software components installed.

CHAPTER 3: TCP/IP

94

Select network component type

You can add all sorts of network components:

- network adapters: quite often, cards to be added in computers, but also PCMCIA cards of parallel port adapters for portables;

- protocols such as TCP/IP, Net-BEUI etc;

- clients, to connect to various networks (Microsoft, Novell, SUN, Banyan-Vines, Digital, IBM etc – after all, Microsoft Networks are not the only ones).

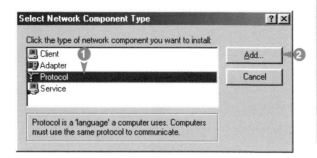

Checklist

1. Click the *Protocol* line.

2. Click *Add*.

Select network protocol

Checklist

1. If you want to use a Microsoft network, click the *Microsoft* line (Windows 95/98 can also accept protocols made to communicate with non-Microsoft networks).

   Click the *TCP/IP* line.

2. Click *OK* to add the
3. protocol.

1. Click the Microsoft line.

2. Click the TCP/IP line.

3. Click OK.

Network

This tab is used to specify the computer name and that of the workgroup.

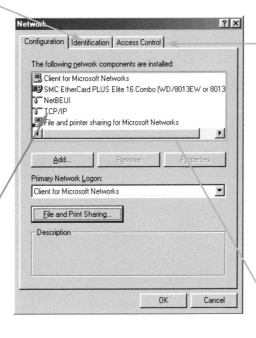

Here you can choose the type of access control that Windows will carry out on users.

Double-click TCP/IP to begin configuration

List of network software components installed: you can see that TCP/IP has been installed.

Now that you have installed the TCP/IP protocol, you must configure it.

Begin this process by double-clicking *TCP/IP.*

It is perfectly possible to have several network protocols and services installed at the same time. Normally, there should be no compatibility problems. You can, for example, have File and printer sharing for Microsoft Networks **working concurrently with** File and Printer sharing for Novell Networks.

Under the *IP Address* tab, you must specify the computer's IP address on the network. The TCP/IP settings cannot be detailed in this book. However, the values given by way of illustration are perfectly suitable for the first machine if you do not need to be connected to an existing LAN. You can choose IP address 10.10.10.2 for the second computer, 10.10.10.3 for the third, and so on, or any other progression.

1 Select *Specify an IP address*.

2 Enter the settings in your possession.

3 Click *OK* to validate.

TCP / IP properties

IP address tab

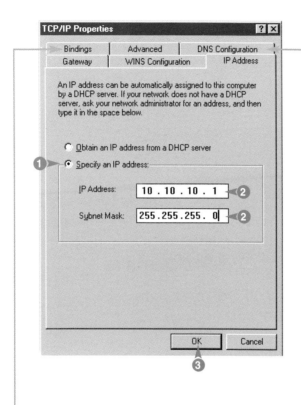

The DNS (domain name server) is essential for Internet service providers. This server stores and converts its client Internet addresses (such as mail@service_provider.co.uk) into IP addresses (such as 10.10.10.1), the only ones that network protocols understand. The DNS Configuration tab is used to indicate the IP address of the provider's DNS server. In our case, no DNS setting is needed.

Used to activate certain services or clients. The link is obvious in a LAN. But when you are connected to the Internet, for example, it is in your interest not to bind 'file and print sharing', in order to increase security and to prevent other Internet users gaining access to your directories.

With TCP/IP, it is highly recommended that you record all settings in a notebook and that you display clearly the IP address on the casing of each computer.

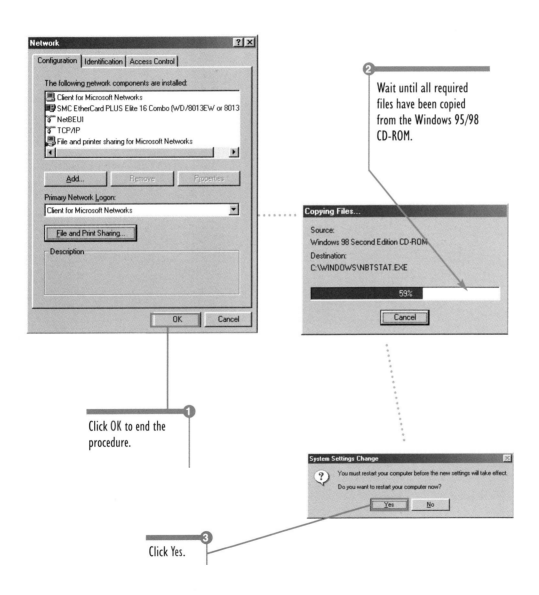

Copying files

Click OK to end the procedure.

Wait until all required files have been copied from the Windows 95/98 CD-ROM.

Click Yes.

Checklist

To finish configuring the TCP/IP protocol, all you have to do is copy from the Windows 95/98 CD-ROM the files that the system needs. You then restart the computer so that these files can be taken into account.

1 Click OK to end the procedure.

2 Wait for the copying of the files from the Windows 95/98 CD-ROM to finish.

3 Click Yes to restart the computer, which is essential for the installation of TCP/IP (or any other protocol) to become effective.

Chapter 4

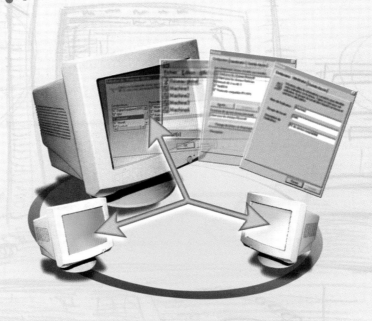

Networking your PCs

Sharing a disk or a folder attached to your PC

Sharing your hard disks means making them accessible to users of other computers on the network via their own machines. You can also share your removable disk drives (**Zip, Syquest, Magneto-Optical**, etc.) and your **CD-ROM** drives. In most cases, for security reasons you will not share an entire hard disk, but only carefully selected folders. To do this, you will have to select the folders, give them a name on the network, and make their access depend on a password. You can, if you wish, choose to have them fully accessible (read and write) or read-only; you can also select different passwords for read-only access and for full access. These are the only access restrictions available under Windows 95 or 98; you will have to acquire and install other network software (some of which, like **LANtastic**, can be installed on Windows 95 or 98) if you want closer access control.

HOW TO

The sharing of a hard disk is carried out from its icon (e.g. *C:*).
To access this icon, double-click *My computer.*

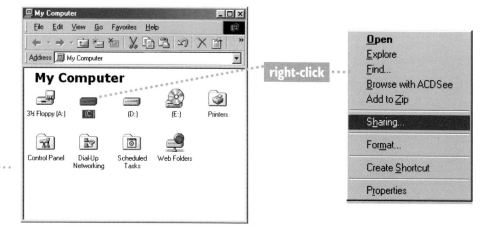

First, if you have not already done so, you need to install the physical network components: cables, tees, plugs, hubs etc. Don't forget to switch all equipment off before you do so. You will also have to restart all PCs connected to the network, and enter the proper user names and passwords, when asked by Windows. Start by connecting only two computers; if everything works, then add the others sequentially. Once again, all wiring must be carried out with the power off.

TIP

Before you can use the hard disks of other PCs, their owners must have activated the global file sharing at Windows level (Start / Settings / Control Panel / Network icon / Configuration tab / File and Print Sharing button). If you have followed our installation procedure, this has already been done.

In a network, the organisation of directories (and their tree structure) that contain work documents is even more important than on stand-alone machines. They must be perfectly homogeneous from one machine to another, otherwise no one will be able to find their way through them. You should always start with a single root directory (e.g. C:\JOHN\PUBLIC\; C:\JOHN\MAIL\). Select one of the PCs in the network on which to make back-ups of all the work documents at the end of the day. Choose a folder such as \DOC in which it will be easy to copy all the personal folders of each person with a simple drag-and-drop procedure. If you map them, do so under the same letter on all computers. Similarly, identify shared printers under the same name on all computers.

Checklist

To access the *Sharing* option of a disk, you must first open its shortcut menu.

1 Double-click the *My Computer* icon.

2 Select the icon of the drive in *My Computer*, and click with the right button of the mouse.

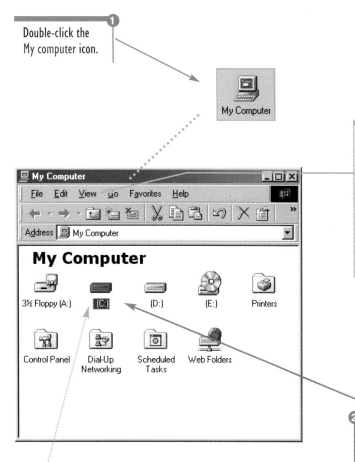

① Double-click the My computer icon.

The view menu is used to select, among other things, whether you wish to display the Toolbar and the Status bar (both optional), whether you want large or small icons and whether you want files sorted in alphabetical order.

② Select the icon of the drive in My computer, and click with the right mouse button.

All drives, fixed or removable, can be shared either totally or partially, by choosing certain folders.

Disk shortcut menu

Right button / Sharing

Same function as when you double-click on the pre-selected icon instead of clicking once.

Gives access to Windows Explorer, which is more complete than My Computer.

The Open function appears in bold because it is the default function, i.e. it is triggered if you double-click on the icon instead of clicking once.

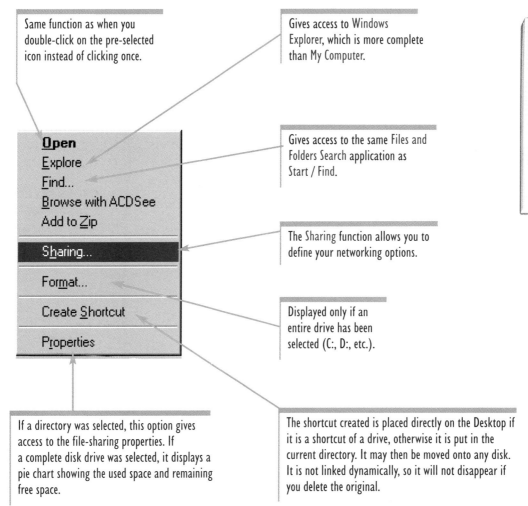

Open
Explore
Find...
Browse with ACDSee
Add to Zip
Sharing...
Format...
Create Shortcut
Properties

Gives access to the same Files and Folders Search application as Start / Find.

The Sharing function allows you to define your networking options.

Displayed only if an entire drive has been selected (C:, D:, etc.).

If a directory was selected, this option gives access to the file-sharing properties. If a complete disk drive was selected, it displays a pie chart showing the used space and remaining free space.

The shortcut created is placed directly on the Desktop if it is a shortcut of a drive, otherwise it is put in the current directory. It may then be moved onto any disk. It is not linked dynamically, so it will not disappear if you delete the original.

Checklist

① Tick *Shared As*.

② Give a name for the network to the hard disk or to the folder that will be shared with the other PCs.

③ Enter a comment that makes it easier to understand who owns this hard disk/directory.

④ Select the level of security desired. The access type *Depends on Password* combines the two preceding options and the users of the network will have *Read-Only* or *Full* access depending on the password they provide.
A password is not compulsory for the first two options and you can leave the entry field blank.

Gives access to a pie chart showing the used space and the remaining free space.

Gives access to standard Windows disk check (ScanDisk) and disk defragmenter utilities.

(C:) Properties   ? X

General | Tools | Sharing

○ Not Shared
① ● Shared As:

   Share Name: [C] ◄②

   Comment: [Fixed Hard disk] ◄③

Access Type:

④ ○ Read-Only
   ○ Full
   ● Depends on Password

Passwords:

   Read-Only Password: [********]

   Full Access Password: [********]

[OK]   [Cancel]   [Apply]

Password Confirmation

1 Enter the two passwords again.

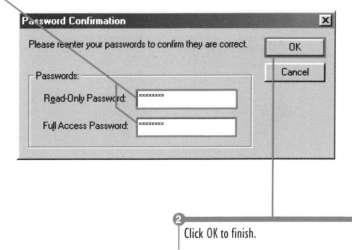

2 Click OK to finish.

Windows 95/98 does not distinguish between uppercase and lowercase in passwords.

Checklist

To avoid any entry error, you are now asked to confirm the two passwords.

1 Enter the two passwords again.

2 Click *OK* to finish.

Passwords are invisible, so they cannot be seen by an inquisitive neighbour.

My Computer

The hand in this icon is telling you that drive C: is now shared.

You are back in front of *My Computer*.

The icon of the disk you decided to share is now showing a hand, confirming that the drive is now shared.

Removing disk or folder sharing

It is very easy to change the conditions under which a hard disk or a folder is shared (such as switching between full access or read-only, or modifying a password): simply follow the same steps, and change the current settings. You may also wish to remove the sharing of a disk drive. However, keep in mind that changes can affect the network and can upset people uninformed of the changes, as they will experience difficulties in trying to access your disks. If possible, do not make such changes while colleagues are connected to your resources; choose to do it when no one is at work.

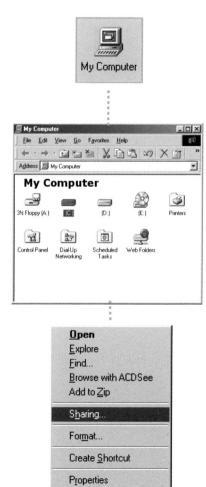

TIP

To avoid cutting off the access of those using your disks through the network, use Net Watcher (for details on how to use this tool, see page 148).

Checklist

To access the *Sharing* option of a disk, you must first open its shortcut menu.

1 Double-click the *My computer* icon.

2 Select the icon of the drive in *My computer*, and click with the right button of the mouse.

1 Double-click the My Computer icon.

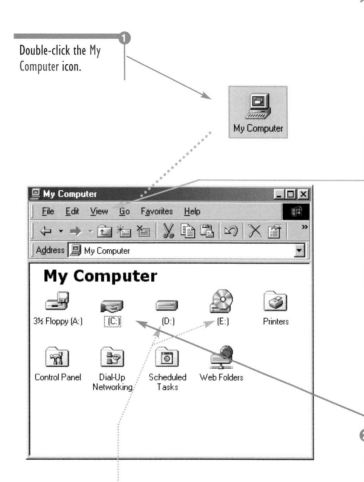

The View menu is used to select, among other options, whether you wish to display the Toolbar or the Status bar (both optional), whether you want large or small icons, and whether you want files sorted in alphabetical order.

2 Select the icon of the drive in My Computer, and click with the right mouse button.

All drives, fixed or removable, can be shared either totally or partially by choosing some of their folders.

Disk shortcut menu

Right button / Sharing

Same action as when you double-click on an icon.

Gives access to Windows Explorer, which is more complete than My Computer.

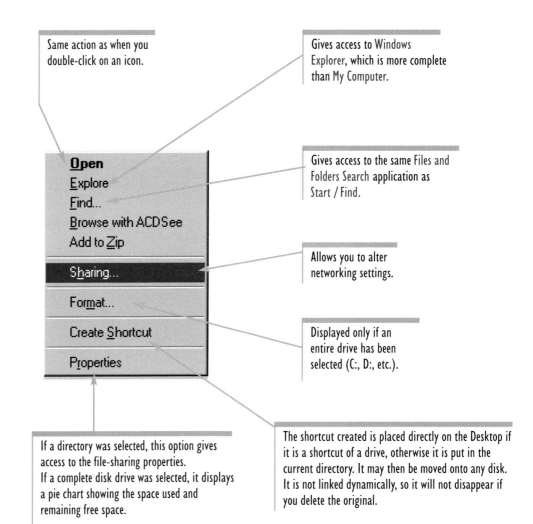

Open
Explore
Find...
Browse with ACDSee
Add to Zip

Sharing...

Format...

Create Shortcut

Properties

The Open function appears in bold because it is the default function, i.e. it is triggered if you double-click on the pre-selected icon.

Gives access to the same Files and Folders Search application as Start / Find.

Allows you to alter networking settings.

Displayed only if an entire drive has been selected (C:, D:, etc.).

If a directory was selected, this option gives access to the file-sharing properties.
If a complete disk drive was selected, it displays a pie chart showing the space used and remaining free space.

The shortcut created is placed directly on the Desktop if it is a shortcut of a drive, otherwise it is put in the current directory. It may then be moved onto any disk. It is not linked dynamically, so it will not disappear if you delete the original.

Disk properties

To remove the sharing of a disk, simply select *Not Shared* and click *OK*.

Gives access to a pie chart showing the space used and the remaining free space.

Gives access to standard Windows disk check (ScanDisk) and disk defragmenter utilities.

Click here to turn file sharing off.

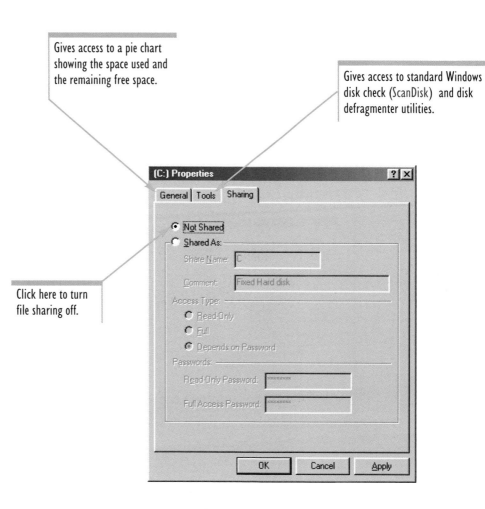

My Computer

You are back in front of *My Computer.*

The icon of the hard disk you decided to stop sharing no longer includes a hand, confirming that the drive is no longer shared.

The hand no longer appears on the icon. This confirms that the disk is no longer shared.

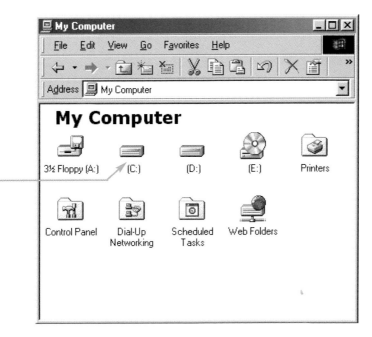

Accessing other computers' disks or folders

Before you can use the hard disks of other **PCs**, you must activate the Windows file- and print-sharing function (*Start* / *Settings* / *Control Panel* / *Network* icon / *Configuration* tab / *File and Print Sharing* button). If you have followed the network installation procedure, this is already done. The owners of the disks must also have activated the sharing of the disks or directories. You must have been told what password (if any) is required, and what sharing restrictions (read and write or read-only) have been imposed.

Please note that we strongly recommend that you map the disks and folders that you wish to access permanently (see Chapter 1). This will save you from having to carry out what can be complex browsing on the network: it is essential if you use non-native (Windows 95/98) applications (non-32–bit), because they are not capable of such browsing.

HOW TO

The *Network Neighborhood* and *My Computer* icons are accessible from the Desktop. To access the Explorer, click *Start*, then *Programs*, then *Windows Explorer*.

Network Neighborhood

Network Neighborhood

Desktop

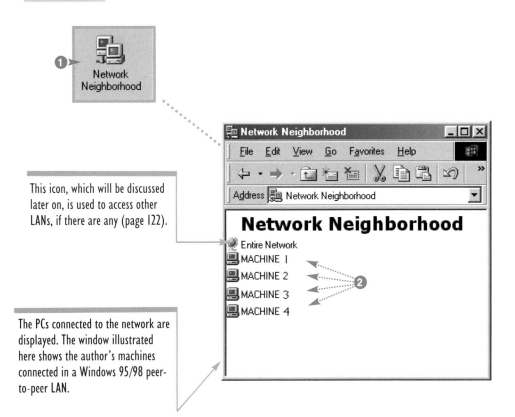

❶ Network Neighborhood

This icon, which will be discussed later on, is used to access other LANs, if there are any (page 122).

The PCs connected to the network are displayed. The window illustrated here shows the author's machines connected in a Windows 95/98 peer-to-peer LAN.

Checklist

A new icon (*Network Neighborhood*) is now on the desktop.

❶ Double-click the *Network Neighborhood* icon.

❷ Double-click a computer icon to browse the corresponding PC.

Press F5 to refresh the list of machines connected and display those connected since this window opened.

Displaying the directories of the selected PC

Name of the selected PC.

To browse on a network computer, select a folder (here, *unit_d1*), then click with the right button of the mouse.

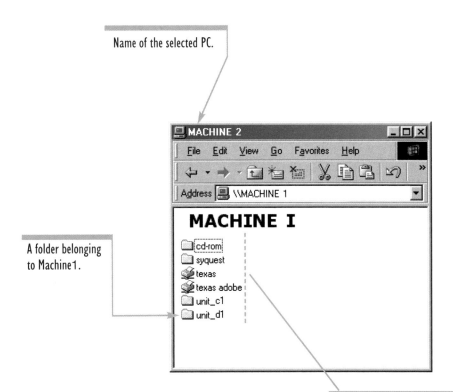

A folder belonging to Machine1.

Shared resources of the PC named Machine1. There are printers too; we will see how to connect to them on page 124.

Map Network Drive

This results in the same action as when you double-click on the pre-selected icon.

Clicking here gives access to Windows Explorer, which is more complete than My Computer.

Open
Explore

Map Network Drive... ◄①

Create Shortcut

Properties

The shortcut created is placed directly on the Desktop if it is a shortcut for a drive, otherwise in the current directory. It may then be moved on to any disk. Warning: it is not linked dynamically, i.e. it will not disappear if you delete the original.

If a directory was selected, this option gives access to the setting of the file sharing. If a complete disk drive was selected, it displays a pie chart showing the used space and remaining free space.

① Click the *Map Network Drive*.

From here you can create an additional drive letter that will enable you to gain direct access to the *drive_d1* directory of *Machine1*, without having to browse from the *Network* icon on the Desktop.

This operation is known as 'mapping' a network resource: it is essential for Windows 3.x (16-bit) applications, because they cannot browse. It is a great time-saver with Windows 95/98.

Checklist

1 Select the letter you want to associate with the resource selected on the network. Windows proposes automatically the first letter available on your computer.

2 Check this option if you want to find this drive letter each time you start the PC.

3 Click OK to confirm.

Select here the letter you want to associate with the resource selected on the network. Windows proposes automatically the first letter available on the computer.

Click OK to confirm.

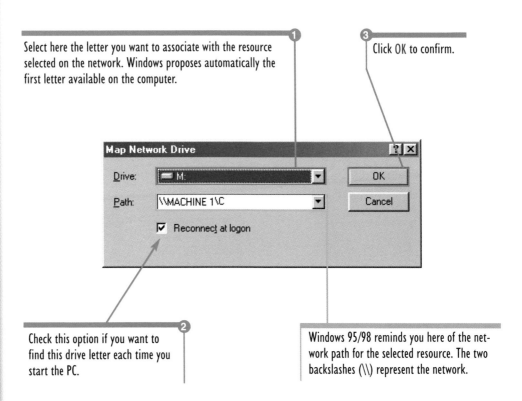

Check this option if you want to find this drive letter each time you start the PC.

Windows 95/98 reminds you here of the network path for the selected resource. The two backslashes (\\) represent the network.

It is good practice to start sufficiently far into the alphabet in attributing network letters (e.g. with H or M) so as to avoid problems if you want to add physical peripherals to your computer (hard disks, CD-ROM drives, ZIP or magneto-optical drive etc.). It is also recommended that you attribute the same letter to the same resource (disk drive or folder) on all computers in the network, otherwise it is easy to lose track of what a letter stands for. For example, we could associate the directory C:\DOCS\STYLES of PC Machine1 with the letter 'U' on all the computers.

This window was displayed automatically as soon as you closed the previous window via the OK button. It displays the contents of *Unit_D1* attached to *Machine1* as if you had browsed through the *Network* icon from the Desktop. You can now browse through folders of the disk that is shared through the network.

Click the X to make the window of the *M* network drive disappear. You will be able to find it again thanks to a new icon created automatically (see page 119).

Files and directories on the new network drive

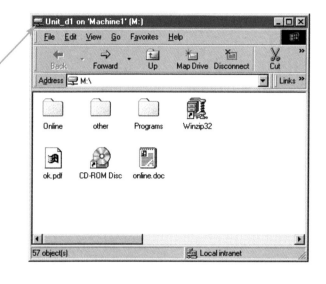

In the system box, you see the letter now associated to \\Machine1\drive_d1.

Note:

Since Windows 95 (and Windows NT4), the term 'folder' has started to replace 'directory'.

Checklist

Notice that a new icon has appeared in *My Computer* and that it cannot be moved.

1. Double-click the *My Computer* icon.

2. *My Computer* now has a new icon with a link to directory *unit_d1* on *Machine1*. Double-click this icon to open the window displayed previously. The cable under the icon tells you that this icon represents a network ressource.

3. Try moving this icon to the *Desktop*: it will not budge!

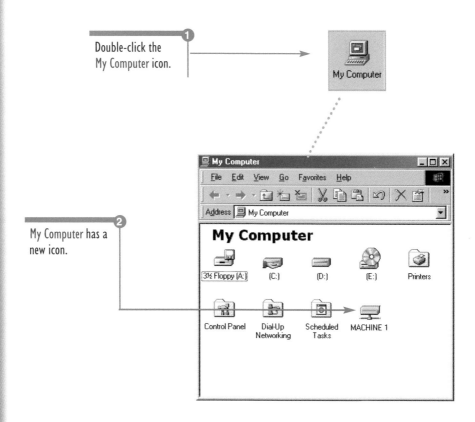

Double-click the My Computer icon.

My Computer has a new icon.

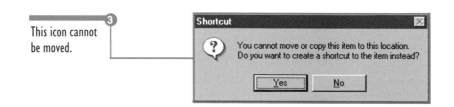

This icon cannot be moved.

Shortcut to a network drive

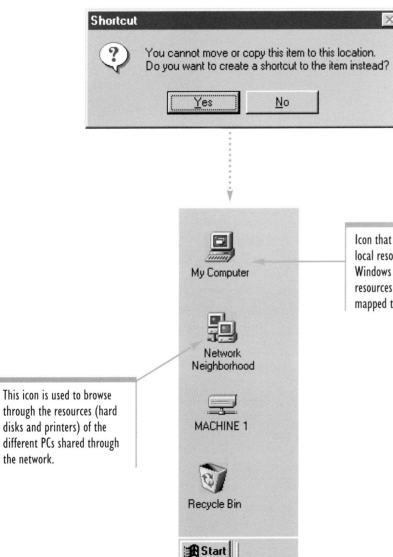

As it is not possible to move the new icon on to the Desktop, Windows proposes automatically creating a shortcut for it. Check that the shortcut appears on the Desktop.

Icon that gives access to the local resources of a PC under Windows 95/98/NT and to resources of other machines mapped through the network.

This icon is used to browse through the resources (hard disks and printers) of the different PCs shared through the network.

Removing a network drive

To remove a network drive, select the icon previously created in *My Computer*, and click the right button of the mouse to remove the link with *unit_d1* icon on *Machine1* (M:). Remember that this action will not delete a shortcut created on the Desktop.

The Open function appears in bold because it is the default function, i.e. it is triggered if you double-click on the icon.

Same action as double-clicking on an icon.

Gives access to Windows Explorer, which is more complete than My Computer.

Gives access to the same Files and Folders Search applications as Start / Find.

Allows you to turn off sharing.

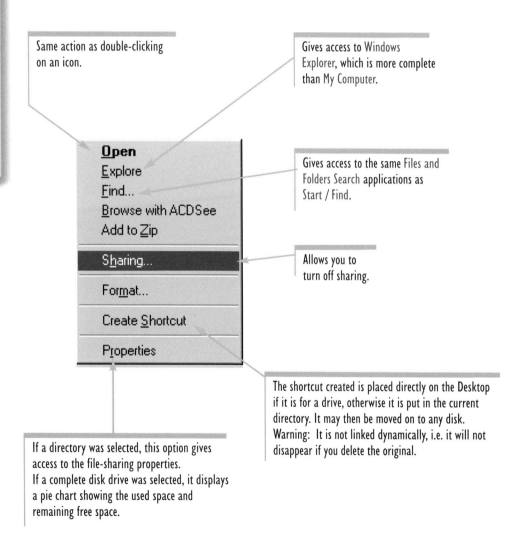

Open
Explore
Find...
Browse with ACDSee
Add to Zip
Sharing...
Format...
Create Shortcut
Properties

The shortcut created is placed directly on the Desktop if it is for a drive, otherwise it is put in the current directory. It may then be moved on to any disk. Warning: It is not linked dynamically, i.e. it will not disappear if you delete the original.

If a directory was selected, this option gives access to the file-sharing properties.
If a complete disk drive was selected, it displays a pie chart showing the used space and remaining free space.

Explorer

Start / Programs / Windows Explorer

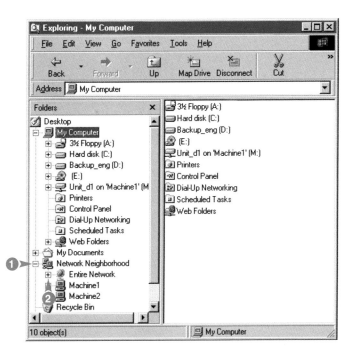

Windows Explorer lets you view all the resources shared through the network.

① Click on the + sign of *Network Neighborhood* (the + sign now becomes a – sign), to view the PCs that belong to the same workgroup as yours.

② Click on the + of the *Entire Network* (the + sign now becomes a – sign), to view the list of workgroups on the Windows 95/98 network and the PCs that are part of them.

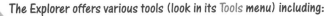

The Explorer offers various tools (look in its Tools menu) including:

– Finding a computer in the network when you know either its name or just part of it. For example, in order to find a computer named Machine4, just enter Ma, or Machine, or chine, etc.

– The option of mapping the hard disk of another PC to a network drive letter.

Explorer

Here you find a disk *unit_d1* which was mapped to *M:*; we can also say that '*M:*' was assigned to the disk *unit_d1* of *Machine1*. The *M:* drive is obviously not a local disk, but only a pointer to the disk *unit_d1* of the PC *Machine1*.

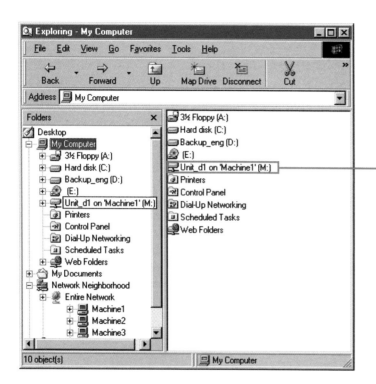

Explorer provides a more global view than the My Computer and the Network Neighborhood icons.

Sharing your printers
Start / Settings / Printers

Sharing your printers means making them accessible to users of other PCs through the network, as if they were connected to their own machines. Please note that there are no network printers in the peer-to-peer networks under Windows (Windows for Workgroups, Windows 95, Windows 98, Windows **NT WorkStation**) as there are for **PCs** networked with a dedicated server: only printers connected to a PC's physical port (usually a parallel port) can be shared. Except in some special cases, they cannot be connected directly to the **LAN** via their Ethernet port, for example.

TIP

Make sure you choose sharing names that make it possible for everyone to find their way in the network, i.e. to know where each printer is located physically.

HOW TO

There are several ways to access the *Printers* icon:

1. Click *Start*, then *Settings*, *Printers*.

Or

2. Click *Start*, *Settings Control Panel* and double-click the *Printers* icon.

Or

3. Double-click the *My Computer* icon on the Desktop, and then double-click the *Printers* icon.

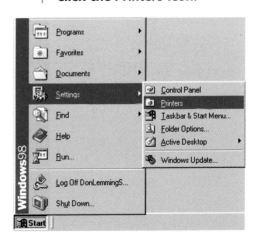

To share printers, you will have to select them, and to give them a name on the network. You can also – if you wish – restrict their accessibility through the use of a password. These are the only access restrictions with Windows 95 or 98. If you want more elaborate restrictions, you will have to acquire and install another network software (some of which, like **LANtastic**, can be installed on top of Windows 95 or 98).

First of all, if you have not already done so, you will have to connect the **PCs** (with the power off) to the network using cables, tees, plugs, hubs etc. You will also have to restart all **PCs** connected to the network and log on with the proper user name and password. Start by connecting only two computers; if everything goes well, then add the other computers sequentially. Remember: always turn the **PCs** off before connecting cables.

Before you can use the printers attached to other PCs, their users must have activated the global file-sharing service (using Start / Settings / Control Panel / Network icon / Configuration tab / File and print sharing button). If you have followed our installation procedure, it has already been done.

Printers

Used to select, among other things, whether you wish to display the Toolbar or the Status bar (both optional), whether you want large or small icons, and whether you want the files sorted in alphabetical order.

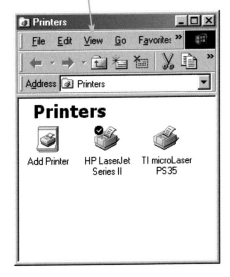

You are going to use the printer shortcut menu in order to share the printer on the network.

The other users will then be able to print on this printer from their PC, provided the correct driver was installed (and configured properly) on their computer.

To share a printer connected to one of your PC's parallel ports, click on that printer's icon.

Click the right button of the mouse.

When you double-click a printer icon, you open that printer's spooler, or print queue file, an area where you can see the printing jobs in progress, with the name of the document, the printing date, etc. From here you can also reorganise printing jobs that have not started yet, as well as pause or purge jobs.

Printer shortcut menu

Right mouse button

Same as double-clicking an icon.

Pauses printing temporarily. Not recommended while print jobs are in progress because you can pause only what the computer is about to send to the printer but not what the printer has already received and stored in its buffer.

Open

Pause Printing

✔ Set as Default

Purge Print Documents

Sharing...

Create Shortcut
Delete
Rename

Properties

If you select this option, further print jobs will be sent automatically to this printer, unless you select another one.

Purges print jobs; same observations as for Pause apply here.

Sharing allows you to pool printers on the LAN.

This gives access to the settings of the selected printer.

The created shortcut is placed automatically on the Desktop. Warning: it is not linked dynamically, i.e. it will not disappear if you delete the original.

You are going to ask Windows to share the printer on the local area network. Select the *Sharing* option.

The Open command appears in bold because it is the default command, i.e. it is triggered if you double-click on the icon.

Properties of the selected printer

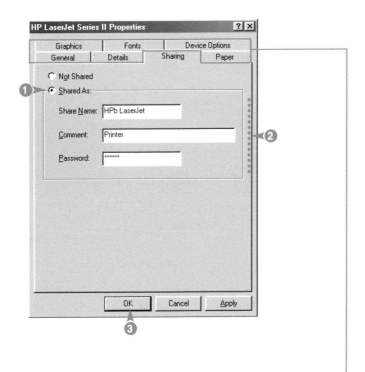

1 Click *Shared As*.

2 Enter settings as you did to share a hard disk: start by specifying the *Share Name* that the other users will see on the network when they choose a printer. Then use the Comment field to specify the physical location of the printer (this is important when several printers are shared through the same network). Finally choose a password if you wish; this is, of course, less important than when sharing hard disks or folders.

3 Click *OK* to confirm.

It is possible to share any hardware or application that uses a printer-type driver, even if it is not a printer. This is the case for faxes, applications such as Adobe Distiller (software that is part of the Acrobat package) and other software from Adobe and other publishers.

The other tabs give access to the printer settings. There are more options than when accessing the properties from an application. Although some settings are identical in all printers, there are many differences between models, in particular between PCL (Printer Control Language, the Hewlett-Packard Laserjet standard) and PostScript printers.

Password confirmation

To avoid keying errors, you are now asked to confirm the password.

1. Enter the password once again.

2. Click *OK* to confirm.

1 Enter the password a second time.

Password Confirmation

Please reenter your password to confirm it is correct.

Password: xxxxx|

OK

Cancel

2 Click OK to confirm.

The passwords are invisible, so they cannot be seen by an inquisitive neighbour.

When you enter a password, make sure that the caps lock is not activated. An LED indicator on the keyboard will tell you whether this function is turned on.

Printers

A hand, under the printer icon, confirms the printer is now shared throughout the network.

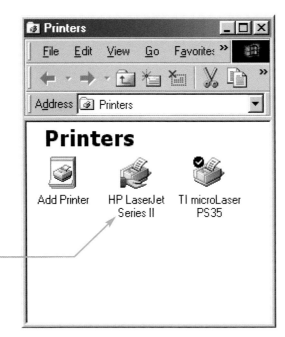

You are now back to the *Printers* window.

The printer icon shows a hand that confirms that it is shared (like the icon of a shared hard disk or folder).

Removing printer sharing

Start / Settings / Printers

You can change the sharing conditions of a printer very easily. All you have to do is follow the same procedure as before, and change the current settings. You can, if you wish, also remove the sharing of a printer as shown below. Just keep in mind that such changes can affect the network and cause a flow of complaints if the users concerned are not properly informed, as they may experience problems accessing your printers. In any event, it is preferable not to proceed to such changes while users are connected to your resources; instead, choose a time when no one is working.

HOW TO

There are several ways to access the *Printers* icon:

1. Click *Start*, then *Settings*, and then *Printers*.

Or

2. Click *Start*, *Settings*, *Control Panel* and then double-click the *Printers* icon.

Or

3. Double-click *My Computer* on the Desktop, then double click the *Printers* icon.

TIP

To avoid cutting off the access of those using your printers via the network, use Net Watcher in order to see who is currently accessing your resources (for details on how to use this tool, see page 148).

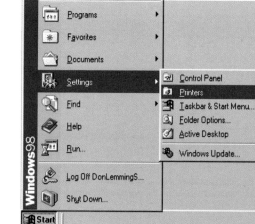

Printers

Used to select, among other things, whether you wish to display the Toolbar or the Status bar (both optional), whether you want large or small icons, and whether you want files sorted in alphabetical order.

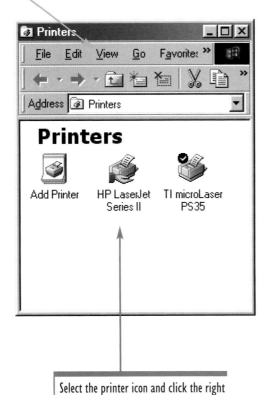

To access the *Sharing* menu of the printer, open its shortcut menu as you did for a hard disk.

Select the icon of the printer you want to stop sharing, then click the right button of the mouse.

Select the printer icon and click the right mouse button.

Printer shortcut menu

You are going to stop sharing a printer on the LAN.

Select the *Sharing* command.

Same as double-clicking an icon.

Pauses printing temporarily. Not recommended while print jobs are in progress because you can pause only what the PC is about to send to the printer, not what the printer has already received and stored in its buffer.

Open

Pause Printing

✔ Set as Default

Purge Print Documents

Sharing...

Create Shortcut

Delete

Rename

Properties

If you select this option, further print jobs will be sent automatically to this printer, unless you select another one.

Purges the print jobs; same observations as for Pause apply here.

Select Sharing to begin process.

The **Open** command appears in bold because it is the default command, i.e. it is obtained if you double-click the icon.

Gives access to the settings of the selected printer.

The shortcut is placed automatically on the Desktop. Warning: it is not linked dynamically, i.e. it will not disappear if you delete the original.

CHAPTER 4: NETWORKING YOUR PCS

Checklist

Removing the sharing of a printer is a simple procedure.

1 Click *Not Shared*.

2 Click *OK* to confirm.

Properties of the selected printer

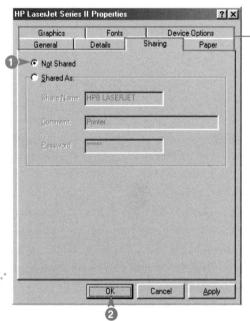

The other tabs give access to the printer settings. There are more options than when accessing the properties from within an application. In any event, although a certain number of settings are identical from one printer to the other, there are many differences between models, in particular between PCL (Printer Control Language, the Hewlett-Packard laserjet standard) and PostScript printers.

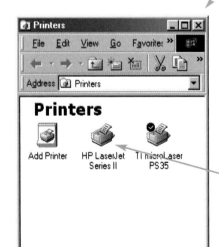

The hand has been removed from the printer icon.

Using network printers

Start / Settings / Printers

Before you can use the printers attached to other **PCs**, their users must have activated the Windows sharing function (*Start / Settings / Control Panel / Network* icon / *Configuration* tab / *File and Print Sharing* button). If they have followed the network installation procedure, this has already been done. They must also have shared individually each of the printers you wish to use, and have communicated any passwords required to access the printers. Using printers shared through the network is the same as if they were attached to your own computer. Obviously, you must keep in mind that this will work only if their PCs are turned on and running under Windows, a problem inevitably encountered with a peer-to-peer type of network, such as that integrated in Windows for Workgroups, Windows 95, Windows 98 or Windows NT WorkStation. Other networks, including a dedicated server, do not pose this problem, as the communication takes place only between your **PC** and the server, which is usually always turned on. Keep in mind that you could have a problem accessing computers through the network if the users are away, the office is closed or the PCs are out of order.

HOW TO

There are several ways to access the *Printers* icon:

1. Click *Start*, then *Settings*, *Printers*.

Or

2. Click *Start*, *Settings*, *Control Panel* and double-click the *Printers* icon.

Or

3. Double-click the *My Computer* icon on the Desktop, and then double-click the *Printers* icon.

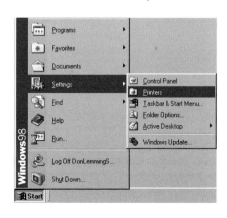

Printers

Used to select, among other things, whether you wish to display the Toolbar or the Status bar (both optional), whether you want large or small icons, and whether you want files sorted in alphabetical order.

Select the icon of a printer *identical* to that shared on the network (same driver).

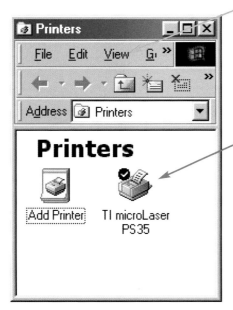

Select the icon of a printer identical to that shared on the network (same driver).

Before you can use a printer shared on the network, you must first install the driver for that printer. In the situation illustrated above, the driver is already installed. This step is essential with Windows 3.x and Windows 95/98. It is not necessary with Windows NT, because this operating system will download the driver from one machine to the other itself.

Printer shortcut menu

Right mouse button

If you are going to change the printer properties, click the *Properties* command.

Same as double-clicking an icon.

Pauses printing temporarily. Not recommended while print jobs are in progress because you can pause only what the microcomputer is about to send to the printer, not what the printer has already received and stored in its buffer.

Open

Pause Printing

✔ Set as Default

Purge Print Documents

Sharing...

Create Shortcut

Delete

Rename

Properties

If you select this option, further print jobs will be sent automatically to this printer, unless you select another one.

Purges the print jobs definitively; same observations as for Pause apply here.

Shares the printer through the network.

The *Open* command appears in bold because it is the default command, i.e. it is triggered if you double-click on the icon.

Click Properties.

The shortcut is placed automatically on the Desktop. Warning: it is not linked dynamically, i.e. it will not disappear if you delete the original.

Printer properties

Details tab

TI microLaser PS35 Properties

| Graphics | Fonts | Device Options | PostScript |
| General | **Details** | Sharing | Paper |

TI microLase 35

Print to the following port:

LPT1: (Printer Port) ▼   Add Port...

Delete Port...

Print using the following driver:

TI microLaser PS35 ▼   New Driver...

Capture Printer Port...   End Capture...

Timeout settings

Not selected: 15 seconds

Transmission retry: 45 seconds

Spool Settings...   Port Settings...

OK   Cancel   Apply

Whatever these values, they will not be taken into account in the network.

The other tabs give access to the printer settings. There are more options than when accessing the properties from an application. Although a certain number of settings are identical in all printers, there are many differences between models, in particular between PCL (the Hewlett-Packard Laserjet standard) and PostScript printers.

Checklist

1. Select *Details*.

2. Click *Add Port*.

Add a printer port

Select this option (this is the default choice).

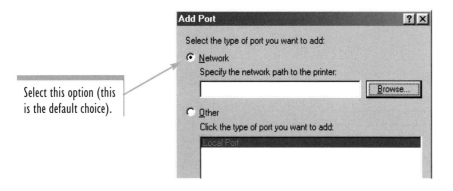

You must now specify the network path to the printer you wish to add. Click the *Browse* button to begin searching.

Browse the network for a printer

Checklist

1. Select a printer connected to another PC. Make sure the driver it requires is already installed on your PC.

2. Click *OK*.

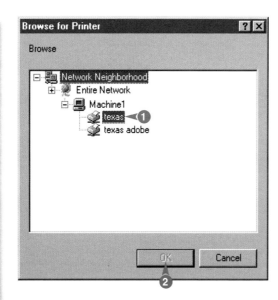

To find out whether the printer selected has the same driver, you may have to walk to the other computer, because the name used to share the printer may not reflect the brand and/or model of the device.

Checklist

Confirm the network printer port.

① Click *OK* to confirm the printer.

Add a port

The network path of the selected printer appears here. The two backslashes (\\) indicate that this printer is not connected directly to your PC (as in the case of hard disks and folders).

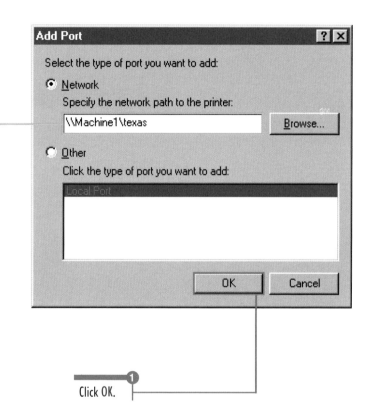

Click OK.

Finish changing the printer properties (once you have made sure that the printing works fine on the printer selected on the network).

Click *OK* to confirm.

.... **Note** ....

Other settings can be changed, but we will not consider them at this point as they do not concern network functions.

Printer properties on the network

The printer path selected on the network has now replaced the previous local port (LPTI, in your case).

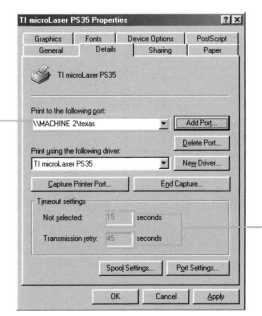

Whatever these values, they will not be taken into account in the network.

The other tabs give access to the printer settings. There are more options than when accessing the properties from an application. Although a certain number of settings are identical in all printers, there are many differences between models, in particular between PCL (the Hewlett-Packard Laserjet standard) and PostScript printers.

A network cable now appears below the icon of the printer that was initially declared as a local drive. It indicates that the printer is accessed through the network even though it can be used by your PC as if it were connected to it. The only difference is that you will have to go and fetch the printed pages from the room where the PC to which the printer is actually connected is located.

Printers

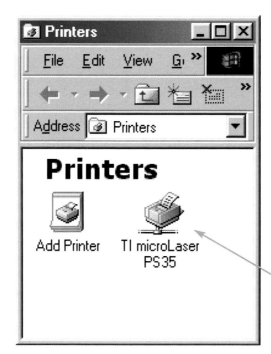

A network cable appears below the icon of the printer, which is not physically connected to your PC. It indicates that this printer is reached through the network.

Printing on a network printer

Start / Programs / Accessories / WordPad

Once printer sharing has been started on some **PCs**, and those wishing to access them have mapped them to their **PCs**, they can use these printers as if they were connected directly to their own machines (ideally, the mapping of printers, as for the mapping of drives or folders, should be done in the same way on all **PCs** involved). Regardless of the speed of your own **PC**, printing time may be affected by the **PC** the printer is attached to. You must also take into account the speed of the network (10 Mb/s or 100 Mb/s) and its load (traffic). This section shows you how to use WordPad, a software application delivered with Windows 95/98 for simple text documents.

HOW TO

To access *WordPad* click *Start*, *Programs*, *Accessories*, *WordPad*.

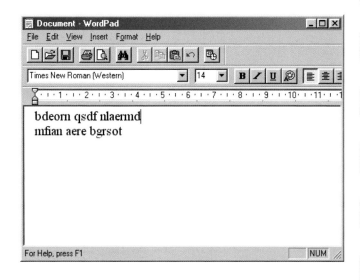

WordPad

Start / Programs / Accessories / Wordpad

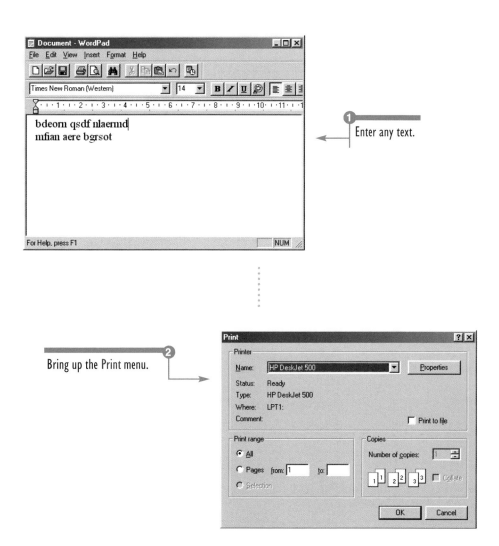

Enter any text.

Bring up the Print menu.

Checklist

If you have followed the instructions correctly, you will have no problems printing.

1 Select the printer you wish to use.

2 Click *OK* to begin printing.

Print / Select printer

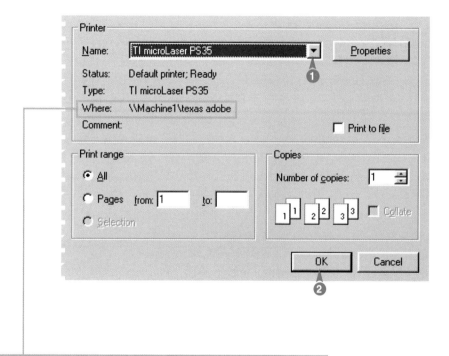

Make sure the selected printer really is a network printer (\\ sign in the Where heading) and that it is the right one; here, it is a printer attached to the PC Machine1, which is shared under the name Texas.

Net Watcher

Start / Programs / Accessories / System Tools / Net Watcher

We mentioned earlier that some users may find it annoying if the owner of a hard disk or a printer decides to change the sharing conditions or, worse, to disable sharing altogether. You must therefore avoid doing this while people are using these resources, because it is always frustrating to interrupt a print job, and it may be dangerous to cut the link with a remote file. Windows 95/98 provides a basic tool, *Net Watcher*, that helps prevent such problems. This application is not necessarily installed on your computer and you may have to add it (*Start / Settings / Control Panel / Add/Remove Programs / Windows Setup / Accessories / Net Watcher*) from the Windows **CD-ROM** before you can go through the steps described in this chapter. It shows which users – and which **PCs** – are connected to your machine's shared resources, and which files on your hard disk they are using. It even allows you to change the sharing conditions at will or to disconnect a user (though this should be avoided).

HOW TO

To access *Net Watcher*, click *Start*, *Programs*, *Accessories System Tools*, *Net Watcher*.

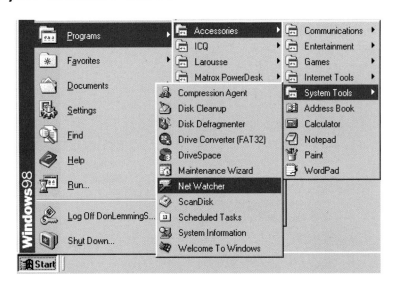

Net Watcher

Disconnects a user.

Adds a share.

Closes a file used (opened) by a user.

Stops a share.

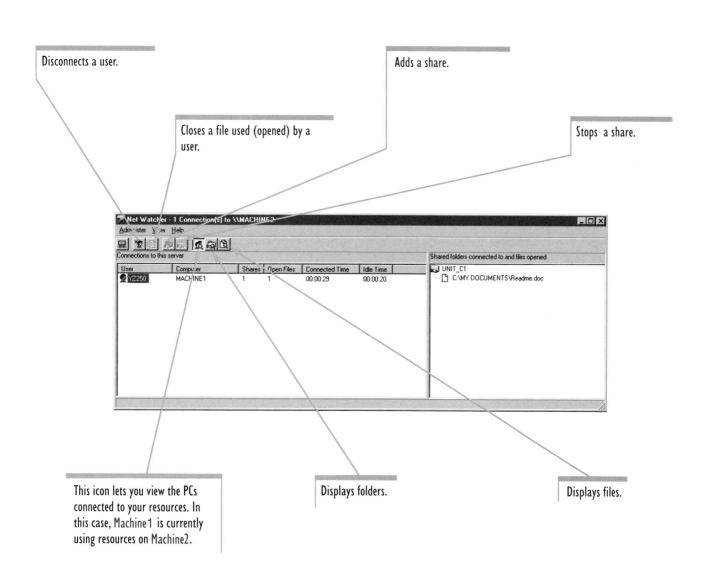

This icon lets you view the PCs connected to your resources. In this case, Machine1 is currently using resources on Machine2.

Displays folders.

Displays files.

Net Watcher / Shared folders

Click this icon to view the PCs connected to your resources.

A user working on Machine1 is using resources on Machine2.

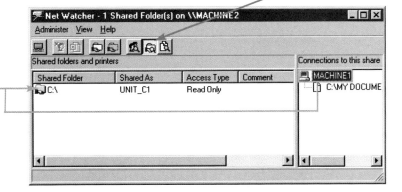

Net Watcher

Disconnect user

In order to disconnect a user, click the second icon from the left on the snapshot above. This step may have regrettable consequences for the other user, which is why the system asks you to confirm the disconnection before it proceeds.

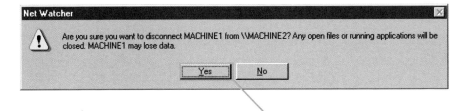

You can still change your mind and cancel the disconnection.

Chapter 5

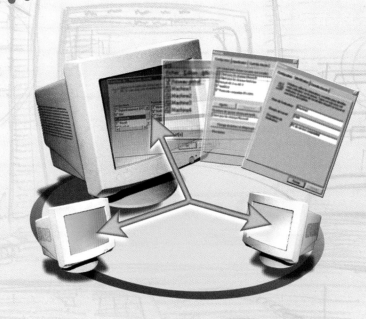

Accessing the Internet

The modem and remote access

The remote-access card you have already installed includes a virtual network card, the *Dial-Up Adapter* card and the **TCP/IP** protocol. It includes the basic remote-connection components, but does not specify how this remote connection will be made. This section will investigate how to install and set the software part of the connection – here, a modem with a telephone line. First, you need to install the remote-access service, configure it and select the modem (from those already installed). It is worth noting that modem connections do not use the **TCP/IP** protocol directly, as they cannot recognise it, but a point-to-point Protocol (**PPP**). This protocol encapsulates the **TCP/IP** data in order to be compatible with modem transmission.

HOW TO

To create the remote network access, proceed as follows:

1. Click *Start*.
2. Click *Settings*.
3. Click *Control Panel*.
4. Double-click the *Add / Remove Programs* icon.
5. Click the *Windows Setup* tab.
6. Click *Communications*.
7. Click *Details*.
8. Click *Dial-Up Networking*.

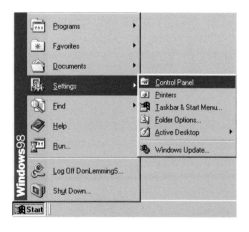

Add/Remove Programs

Properties for Add/Remove Programs

Windows Setup tab

Double-click *Add / Remove Programs*, to install the communication components.

① Click the *Windows Setup* tab.

② Double-click *Communications*.

③ Click *Details* to find out more about the components on your machine.

This tab is used mainly to uninstall applications that follow the Windows 95/98 conventions.

Add/Remove Programs Properties ? ✕

Install/Uninstall | Windows Setup | Startup Disk |

To add or remove a component, select or clear the check box. If the check box is shaded, only part of the component will be installed. To see what's included in a component, click Details.

Components:

☐ 🖰 Accessibility	0.0 MB	
☐ 🖰 Accessories	0.0 MB	
☑ 🖰 Address Book	1.5 MB	
☑ 🖰 Communications	1.2 MB	
☐ 🖰 Desktop Themes	0.0 MB	

Space used by installed components: 8.4 MB
Space required: 0.0 MB
Space available on disk: 1409.4 MB

┌ Description ─────────────────────────────────────
│ Includes accessories to help you connect to other computers
│ and online services.
│
│ 1 of 9 components selected   Details...
└──

Have Disk...

OK   Cancel   Apply

Applications that do not follow the Windows 95/98 conventions must be uninstalled by their own uninstall program (Start/ Programs) if it exists. Otherwise, everything must be done manually. All the files installed by the application, as well as entries in files.INS and the configuration registry, must be removed.

Checklist

The Internet is a remote network, so you must make sure that the access service to this type of network is installed.

1 Tick *Dial-Up Networking* if this option is not already ticked.

2 Click *OK*.

Allows a connection between two PCs connected through a parallel cable. A conventional printer cable will not do, unless it is a two-way cable: only two computers can be connected by this method.

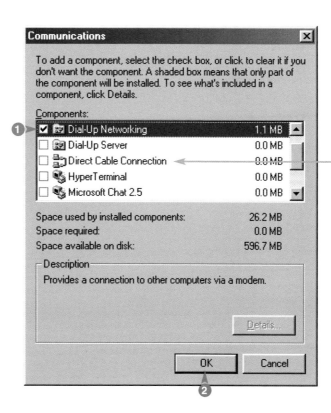

The number of components in the list can vary between versions of Windows. However, most importantly, the Dial-Up Networking is present in all cases.

Properties for Add/Remove Programs

Windows Setup tab

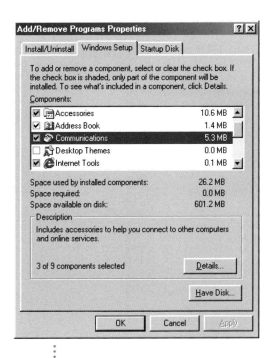

Add/Remove Programs Properties

Install/Uninstall | Windows Setup | Startup Disk

To add or remove a component, select or clear the check box. If the check box is shaded, only part of the component will be installed. To see what's included in a component, click Details.

Components:

☑ 🖥 Accessories	10.6 MB	▲
☑ 📇 Address Book	1.4 MB	
☑ 🖳 Communications	5.3 MB	
☐ 🎨 Desktop Themes	0.0 MB	
☑ 🌐 Internet Tools	0.1 MB	▼

Space used by installed components: 26.2 MB
Space required: 0.0 MB
Space available on disk: 601.2 MB

Description
Includes accessories to help you connect to other computers and online services.

3 of 9 components selected   Details...

Have Disk...

OK   Cancel   Apply

Copying Files...

Source:
Windows 98 Second Edition CD-ROM

Destination:
Scanning ...

75%

Cancel

Once you have selected *Dial-Up Networking*, a number of files must be copied from the Windows CD-ROM. Once you click *OK*, files are copied from the Windows 95 CD-ROM to the hard disk.

Remote-access settings

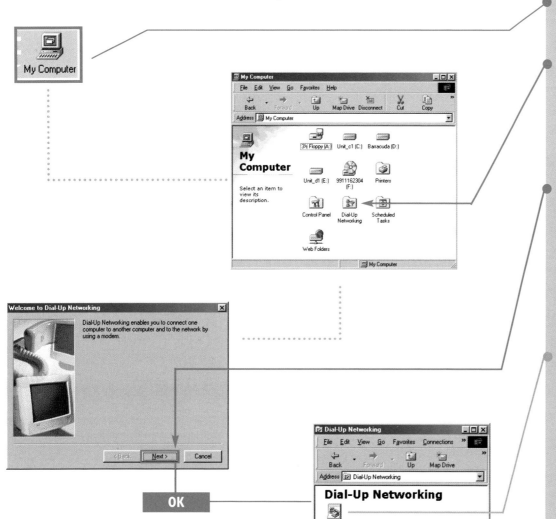

Double-click *My Computer*.

Double-click *Dial-Up Networking*.

Click the *Next* button of this window that appears for the first time.

The next time you double-click the *Dial-Up Networking* icon in the *Control Panel*, this window will appear and you will have to click on the *Make New Connection* icon to continue.

Make new connection

Enter here a name for the connection.

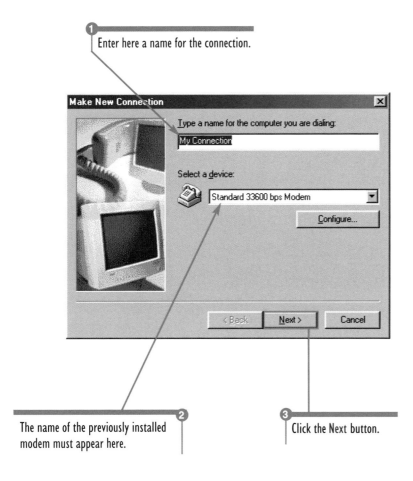

The name of the previously installed modem must appear here.

Click the Next button.

1 Enter here the name you wish to give to the connection.

2 The name of the previously installed modem must appear here. If there are several modems, you must choose the one you wish to use for the Internet connection (another, slower, modem may be reserved for another telephone line, for receiving faxes, etc.).

3 Click the *Next* button.

Checklist

1 Enter here the area code of the computer to call or select it from the attached menu. This is not very important, however, because you are going to disable it later on.

2 Enter here the telephone number used to connect to the ISP's server.

3 You can choose United Kingdom if you are in that country, but it is not very important as you will disable it later on.

4 Click *Next*.

ISP's telephone number

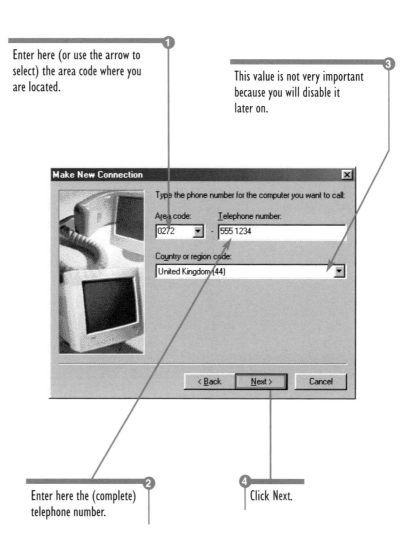

Enter here (or use the arrow to select) the area code where you are located.

This value is not very important because you will disable it later on.

Enter here the (complete) telephone number.

Click Next.

Make New Connection

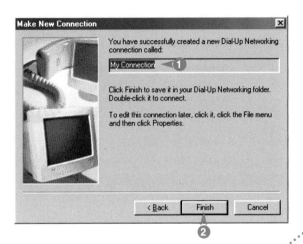

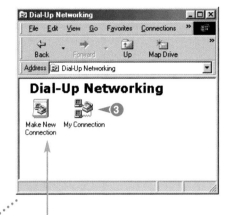

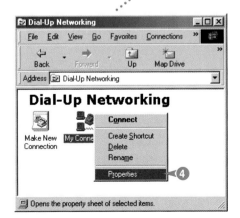

Double-click on this icon every time you want to create a different remote connection, for instance when you connect to another ISP telephone number, or if you have several ISPs.

Checklist

1. You see here the name you have previously chosen for your modem Internet connection. You cannot change this name at this stage of the procedure.

2. Click *Finish* to create the icon that will be used to connect to the Internet through the modem connection.

3. The icon has been created. Select it, and click the right button of the mouse.

4. Click *Properties* from the menu that appears.

Connection settings

Click here to enter your ISP server properties.

Untick this box.

Modem settings.

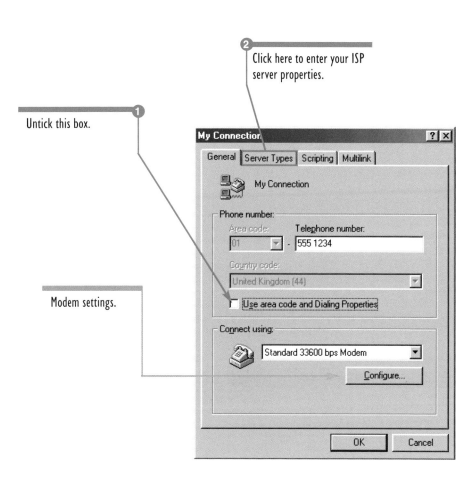

Options and protocols

This option is of no use when you connect to an Internet service provider (ISP); it is used when you log on to your company's LAN by modem (tele-working).

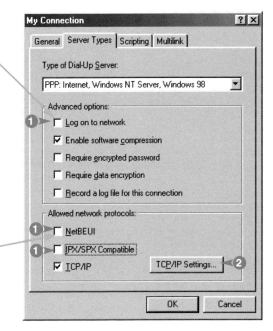

The NetBEUI network is of no use with the Internet; it is used when you access a LAN that uses NetBEUI via a remote connection.

The IPX/SPS protocol is essential when you make a remote connection to access NetWare (Novell) LANs up to version 4.x; as from version 5.x, NetWare can work under TCP/IP.

Checklist

1. Untick these options, which are unnecessary in the case of a connection to the Internet by a modem.

2. Click the *TCP/IP settings* button.

① Leave this box ticked by default (see note below).

② Tick this box to force the use of a particular DNS (domain name server).

③ Enter the TCP/IP address(es) of your ISP in these fields (this has already been done under another heading but you have to do it all over again here).

④ Click *OK* to finish.

Select this option (default choice).

Tick this option.

Enter the IP address of your ISP's domain name servers (primary and secondary).

Click OK.

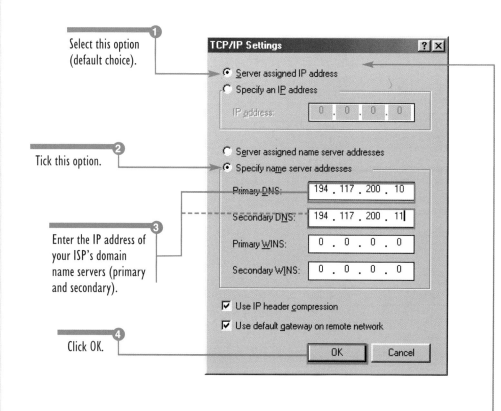

TCP/IP Settings

① ☉ Server assigned IP address
   ○ Specify an IP address
     IP address: 0 . 0 . 0 . 0

② ○ Server assigned name server addresses
   ☉ Specify name server addresses
     Primary DNS: 194 . 117 . 200 . 10
     Secondary DNS: 194 . 117 . 200 . 11
     Primary WINS: 0 . 0 . 0 . 0
     Secondary WINS: 0 . 0 . 0 . 0

☑ Use IP header compression
☑ Use default gateway on remote network

    OK   Cancel

Note: ISP provides a different IP address (type 123.123.123.123) for your PC at the beginning of every connection. In the case of some professionnal applications, ISPs can provide a fixed address (which is much more expensive); if this is your case, tick Specify an IP address and enter that address.

Finish configuring Internet connection

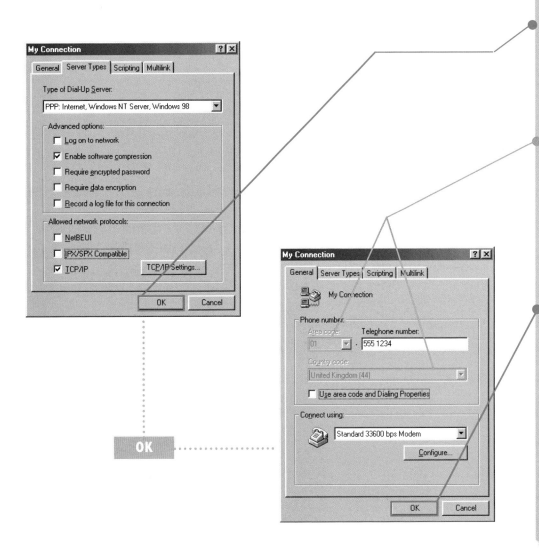

When the My Connection window appears, click *OK* to finish configuring your Internet connection.

You can see that the values initially entered here are now disabled (grey).

Click to close the Internet connection configuration dialogue box.

Sharing your Internet access with other PCs

Settings of the PC that shares its access with others

The second edition of Windows 98 features various improvements: Y2K updates, new peripherals, Internet Explorer, Outlook Express 5 etc. There is also a new software component for sharing the Internet connection of a **PC** with other **PCs** already connected to the same Windows 95/98 peer-to-peer **LAN**. One telephone line, one modem and one subscription/account with an Internet service provider will then suffice to connect all the **PCs**. However, designed essentially for home use, this software component does not increase the bandwidth of your connection and you must not expect to connect successfully a dozen **PCs** to the same modem at the same time! This software component is neither a firewall nor a proxy: it cannot accelerate the reading speed of documents already read by members of your network, restrict access (for your children, for instance) or provide protection against external intrusions (takeovers, information bootlegging, viruses etc.) any more than your current connection can. Finally, it can function only with the **TCP/IP** protocol, and automatically assigns **IP** addresses starting with 192.168.

HOW TO

To add the *Internet access sharing* component, you must access the *Add/Remove Programs* icon; you can then either:

1. Click *Start*, *Settings* and *Control Panel*

Or

2. Double-click the *My Computer* icon (on the Desktop), and then the *Control Panel* icon.

TIP

Internet connection sharing is carried out in two steps: 1. You must install the special component, enter certain settings, and check a number of things on the PC that is to share its Internet access (called the 'host'). 2. You must then configure each of the PCs granted shared access (referred to as 'stations').

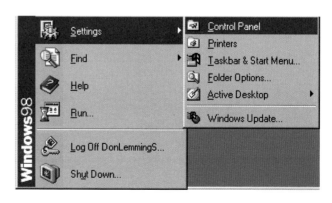

Adding sharing component (1)

Windows Setup tab

Click the Windows Setup tab.

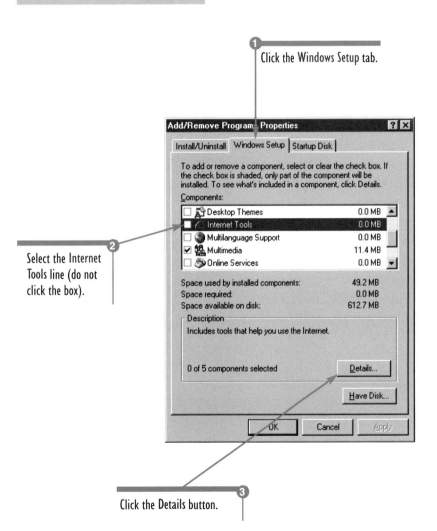

Select the Internet Tools line (do not click the box).

Click the Details button.

Checklist

1 Once you have put the original Windows CD-ROM in the correct drive, double-click the *Add/Remove Programs* icon and select the *Windows Setup* tab.

2 Select the Internet Tools line in the menu.

3 Click on the *Details* button to find out more.

First of all, format a disk ... you will be asked to use it later. Label it as follows: 'Windows 98, Second Edition, Internet connection sharing, Station diskette'.

Internet tools

Checklist

From this dialogue box, you are going to install the *Internet Connection Sharing* software component. Take the opportunity to have a look at the various other components that might be of use to you later, but do not install them now.

1 Tick the *Internet Connection Sharing* box.

2 Click *OK* to confirm.

3 The computer will then ask you to click OK in order to proceed to an Internet Connection Sharing Wizard.

Click the box (not the text!) of the Internet Connection Sharing line.

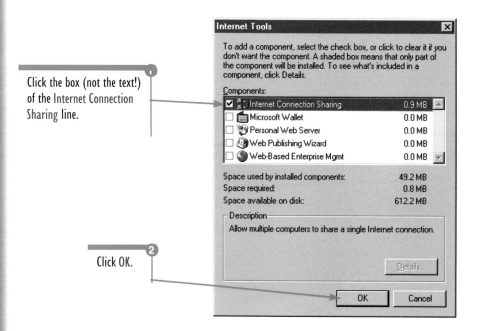

Click OK.

Click OK.

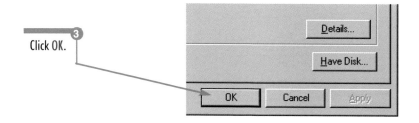

Creating a diskette for the stations (1)

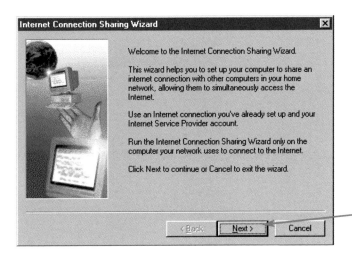

Click Next.

Click Next.

You will need an empy formatted diskette (the one we recommended that you prepare earlier).

Checklist

1. Insert the previously formatted diskette you labelled 'Windows 98, Second Edition, Internet connection sharing, Station diskette'. Click *OK*.

2. When the diskette is ready, remove it from the drive and keep it in a safe place; you will need it to set up every PC that will want to use the shared Internet access.

3. Click *Finish*.

4. Click *Yes* to restart the PC; this operation is essential to take into account the new network settings and to activate the *Internet Connection Sharing*.

Creating a diskette for the stations (2)

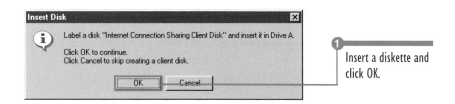

① Insert a diskette and click OK.

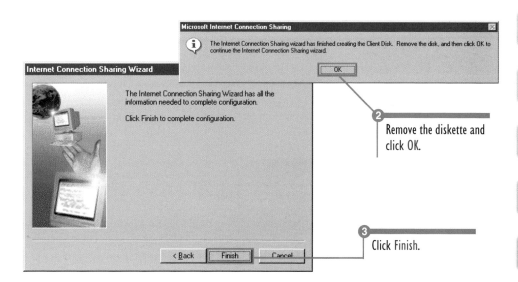

② Remove the diskette and click OK.

③ Click Finish.

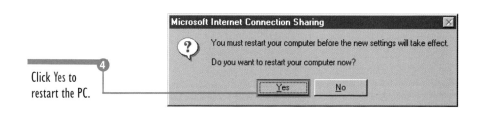

④ Click Yes to restart the PC.

Activating sharing

Control Panel / Internet Options

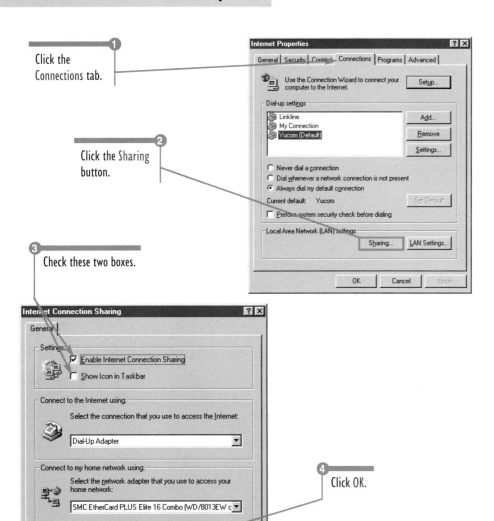

Click the Connections tab.

1

Click the Sharing button.

2

Check these two boxes.

3

Internet Properties   ? X

General | Security | Content | **Connections** | Programs | Advanced |

Use the Connection Wizard to connect your computer to the Internet.   Setup...

Dial-up settings

Linkline
My Connection
Yucom (Default)

Add...
Remove
Settings...

◯ Never dial a connection
◯ Dial whenever a network connection is not present
◉ Always dial my default connection

Current default: Yucom   Set Default

☐ Perform system security check before dialing

Local Area Network (LAN) settings

Sharing...   LAN Settings...

OK   Cancel   Apply

Internet Connection Sharing   ? X

General |

Settings:

☑ Enable Internet Connection Sharing

☐ Show Icon in Taskbar

Connect to the Internet using:

Select the connection that you use to access the Internet:

Dial-Up Adapter   ▼

Connect to my home network using:

Select the network adapter that you use to access your home network:

SMC EtherCard PLUS Elite 16 Combo (WD/8013EW c ▼

4

Click OK.

OK   Cancel   Help

Double-click the *Internet Options* icon on the *Control Panel*, and then:

1 Click the *Connections* tab.

2 Click the *Sharing* button under *LAN Settings* frame.

3 In the new window that appears, click the *Enable Internet Connection Sharing* and *Show Icon in Taskbar*.

4 Click *OK*.

5 Click the *OK* button of the Internet properties dialogue box.

6 A new icon now appears on the taskbar: it is used to enable and disable the connection-sharing.

Checklist

Before setting up the 'stations' that will use the shared Internet access, you should check a number of parameters.

Double-click the *Network* icon in the *Control Panel* and click the *TCP/IP (domestic)* line that has the name of the network adapter installed in your PC.

1. Select the *IP Address* tab.

2. Check that you have exactly what is shown in the screen capture, regardless of your previous settings.

3. Click *OK*, then confirm that you want to restart Windows.

Verification

Control Panel / Network icon

Select the IP Address tab.

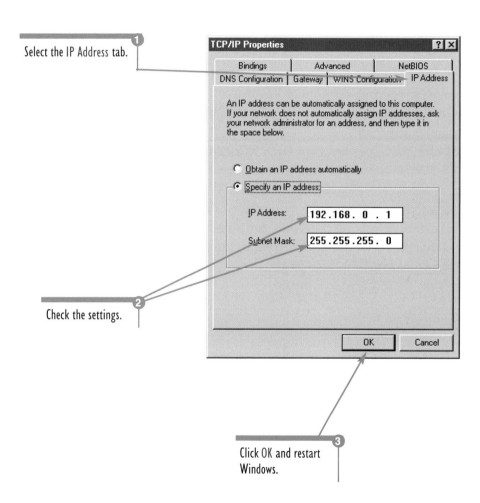

Check the settings.

Click OK and restart Windows.

Configuring PCs to use shared Internet access

In this second step, you are going to configure the PCs that should be able to access the Internet through the host (gateway) configured in the previous step. Each of the PCs will then be connected directly through the peer-to-peer **LAN**, i.e. they will not need their own modem, telephone line or remote access card. Whereas the second edition of Windows 98 is required on the Host, the other can run Windows 98, First Edition, or even Windows 95. You must make sure, however, that **TCP/IP** has been installed on each of the PCs (remember that Windows 95 installs **NetBEUI** by default) and that a Netscape or Internet Explorer, Version 3 or higher, is available. Finally, the original Windows **CD-ROM** must be inserted in the drive before you start. You will enter a few simple parameters on each station, run the executable program file that is now on the diskette prepared beforehand, then check a number of other parameters. The last page shows you how to use the Internet connection, which is very simple.

HOW TO

To enter the necessary settings you must first access the *Network* icon, which can be done in two ways:

1. Click *Start*, *Settings*, *Control Panel*;

Or

2. Double-click the *My Computer* icon (on the Desktop) and then the *Control Panel* icon.

TIP

Leave all your networked PCs on (host and stations alike) while you carry out these operations. This will be absolutely essential when you are asked to run the executable program file on the prepared diskette. It is needed to connect to the host and will dynamically assign an IP address to it.

Setting TCP/IP (1)

IP address tab

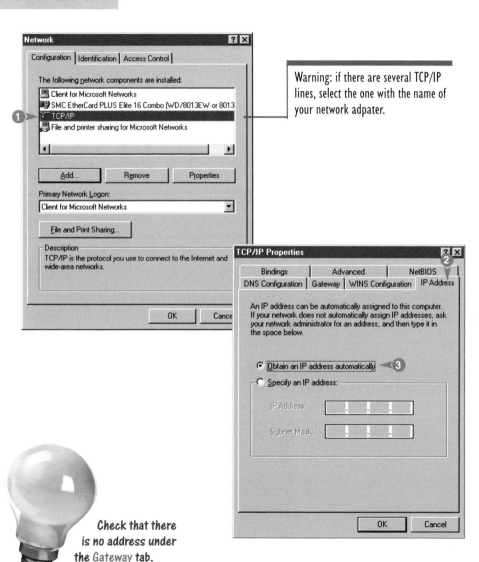

Warning: if there are several TCP/IP lines, select the one with the name of your network adpater.

Check that there is no address under the Gateway tab.

Setting TCP/IP (2)

DNS & Wins Configuration tabs

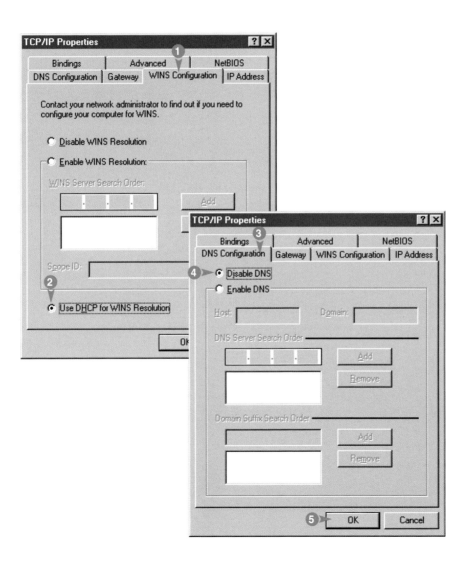

Checklist

1. Click the WINS Configuration tab.

2. Click Use DHCP for WINS Resolution.

3. Click the DNS Configuration tab (but do not click OK yet).

4. Click Disable DNS.

5. Finally, click OK to confirm all settings, and then the OK button of the Network dialogue box, to close it.

Checklist

Insert the diskette you have prepared and labelled 'Windows 98, Second Edition, Internet connection sharing, Station diskette' in the diskette drive. Then check that the host is turned on.

1 Double-click the *icsclset.exe* icon.

2 Click *Next* in the *Browser Setup Wizard* and on the button that is then displayed.

Browser Setup Wizard

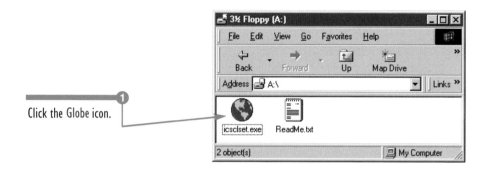

Click the Globe icon.

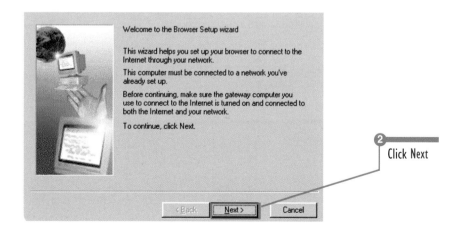

Click Next

Using the special diskette (2)

Browser Setup Wizard

Do not click the checkbox. Click *Finish* to restart your PC (*Start* / *Shut down* / *Restart*).

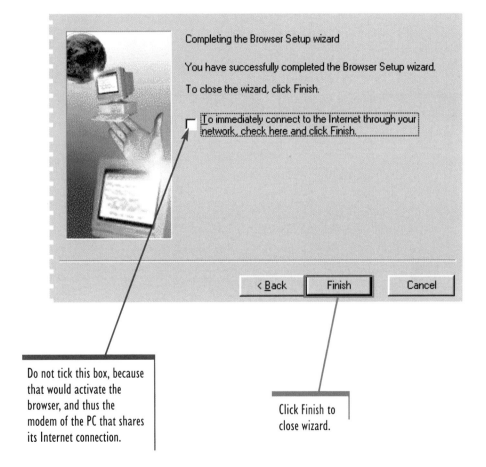

Completing the Browser Setup wizard

You have successfully completed the Browser Setup wizard.

To close the wizard, click Finish.

To immediately connect to the Internet through your network, check here and click Finish.

| < Back | Finish | Cancel |

Do not tick this box, because that would activate the browser, and thus the modem of the PC that shares its Internet connection.

Click Finish to close wizard.

Store the diskette in a safe place; you will need it to set up each PC (Station) that needs to access the Internet via the host (gateway).

Checklist

You must check the TCP/IP settings on each PC that uses the shared Internet connection through the Windows network. To do this, use Winipcfg.exe (*Win* for Windows; *ip* for TCP/IP; *cfg* for configuration), a tool included in Windows 95 and 98 but not installed by Microsoft in the *Start / Programs* menu (probably because it is somewhat technical).

① Enter its name correctly. It is not easy to spell, so double-check what you typed before you click the *OK* button.

② Click *OK*.

③ Click *More Info* at the bottom right: a more detailed window will appear.

Verifying TCP/IP with Winipcfg.exe (1)

Start / Run...

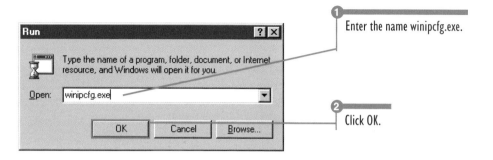

① Enter the name winipcfg.exe.

② Click OK.

③ Click More Info.

Verifying TCP/IP with Winipcfg.exe (2)

Host Information

Host Name	Machine2
DNS Servers	192.168.0.1
Node Type	Broadcast
NetBIOS Scope Id	
IP Routing Enabled	WINS Proxy Enabled
NetBIOS Resolution Uses DNS	

Ethernet Adapter Information

Intel EtherExpress 16 Miniport

Adapter Address	00-AA-00-B3-01-FA
IP Address	192.168.0.2
Subnet Mask	255.255.255.0
Default Gateway	192.168.0.1
DHCP Server	192.168.0.1
Primary WINS Server	
Secondary WINS Server	
Lease Obtained	01 18 00 08:07:41
Lease Expires	01 19 00 08:07:41

OK   Release   Renew   Release All   Renew All

Click OK when you have checked the settings.

Verify that the bottom frame (Ethernet Adapter Information) contains the following information:

A The selection field refers to the network adapter that is actually installed in your PC.

B The IP address starts with 192.168.0; it can be:

192.168.0.2 or

192.168.0.3 or

192.168.0.4 or

192.168.0.5 etc.

C The *Default Gateway* and *DHCP Server* addresses have the value 192.168.0.1. The gateway is the PC that shares its Internet access with the others; a DHCP server is a feature that enables a PC to attribute dynamically IP addresses to the PCs that use its shared Internet connection.

If you have carried out all the steps carefully, the shared connection is now operational.

You connect to the host (gateway) through the *Dial-Up Adapter* icon. Then all you have to do on the stations is run a Web browser or Internet message application, and the modem of the host (gateway) connects to your Internet service provider.

In some cases, the connection sharing doesn't work automatically. You then have to establish the connection from the PC with the modem.

The connection sharing is enabled by default: however, if you wish to disable it temporarily, simply click its icon on the taskbar, then click the *Disable Internet Connection Sharing* line.

Using the Internet Connection Sharing

Sharing icon in the taskbar

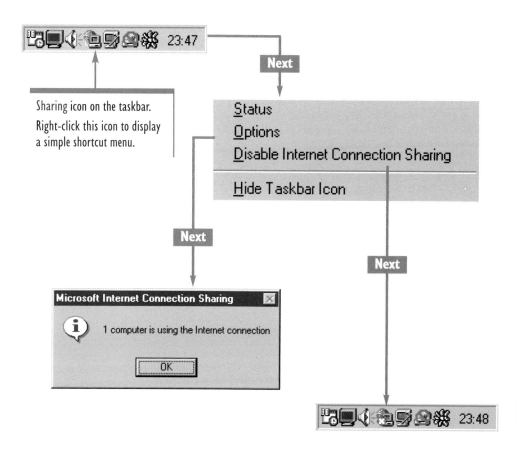

Sharing icon on the taskbar. Right-click this icon to display a simple shortcut menu.

Next

Status
Options
Disable Internet Connection Sharing

Hide Taskbar Icon

Next

Next

Microsoft Internet Connection Sharing

ⓘ 1 computer is using the Internet connection

OK

The snapshots on this page come from the PC that shares its Internet connection.

Glossary

Glossary

10 Base 2 (thin Ethernet)

10 Base 2 was one of the most widespread Ethernet cabling standards because it was economical and very easy to install. It uses a coaxial cable (a type of cable consisting of a central wire surrounded by braided insulation, similar to the cabling used by the cable television industry). This type of cable does not use a hub concentrator.

10 Base F

Local area networks are interconnected not only by copper cabling but also (albeit far less frequently) by fibre optic cables. 10 Base F is the fibre optic cabling standard used with the Ethernet.

10 Base T

10 Base T is the name given to Ethernet 10 Mbps cable that uses an (unshielded) twisted pair cable. Every machine and peripheral on the network (in particular PCs and printers) is connected to one of the inputs of a concentrator called a hub. The two ends of these cables connect by means of male RJ45 connectors. The network adapters used must therefore be equipped with a female RJ45 connector.

10 Mbps, 100 Mbps

The maximum speed (measured in megabits per second) of Ethernet and Fast Ethernet local area networks respectively. In practice, this speed is much slower and depends on the volume of traffic on the network.

Backbone

A backbone is a high speed connection serving as the main communication line of the network. For example, a 100 Mbps Ethernet connection can serve as the backbone for multiple 10 Mbps networks.

Coaxial cable

In local area networks, coaxial cables look like the cables of TV antennas. They are composed of a central wire surrounded by insulation and a grounded shield of braided copper wire. This shield is in turn covered by a layer of plastic insulation.

Collisions

Ethernet networks generate collisions, because there is no 'traffic officer' to control the flow of data transmissions. Such collisions are not dangerous for the network because they are easily managed by the system. They do slowdown the speed of the network, however. Every time a collision occurs, Ethernet sends back the data that have been involved in that collision.

Desktop model computers

Desktop model computers are PCs for office use; the other machines in the network are servers or workstations. A Network Client can be installed on a Desktop or on a workstation.

Dial-up

This refers to temporary connections obtained by calling a telephone number, as when connecting to the Internet via a modem. Local area network connections are not dial-up connections, because they are permanent.

Dial-up adapter

A virtual networking card, which is nonetheless configured somewhat like a real card. It is the software interface that allows you to gain remote access to a network (via modem).

DNS

DNS is a data query service used to translate hostnames into Internet addresses. The 'name servers' store the TCP/IP (Transmission Control Protocol/Internet Protocol) addresses on the one hand, and the Internet addresses known to all on the other hand, and maintain the two in matched pairs in a way that is transparent to users. The Internet addresses of users are easier to remember and accept letters, as everyone knows (example: amazon.com), while the TCP/IP addresses are composed exclusively of groups of digits separated by dots.

Ethernet

The most widespread local area network in the world today. The basic Ethernet version has a maximum speed of 10 Mbps, but there are versions with speeds of 100 Mbps and 1,000 Mbps. Most recent computers are fitted with an Ethernet connector as standard.

Fast Ethernet

Fast Ethernet, also known as 100 Mbps Ethernet, is the name given to a version ten times faster than basic Ethernet. Fast Ethernet does not accept coaxial cabling and requires specific network adapters and hubs.

Hub

A hub is a box, autonomous or drawing power from the mains, which is used as the connection point for cables coming from the servers or client stations used by the network community. This box is equipped with female RJ45 connectors.

Intranet

An Intranet is a local network that uses all the protocols and tools of the Internet. An Intranet can be described as a private Internet.

IPX/SPX (Internetwork Packet Exchange/Sequenced Packet Exchange)

Protocol specific to the Novell's NetWare operating system. It is not found anywhere else.

LANtastic

LANtastic is a peer-to-peer local network operating system, similar to but more sophisticated than the Windows 95/98 systems.

Login

The 'User name' you enter when you connect to a network (local area network, Internet, Intranet, extranet).

NetBEUI

The standard transport protocol in Microsoft networks, displaced by TCP/IP (Transmission Control Protocol/Internet Protocol) with the Internet boom. TCP/IP is installed by default with Windows 98.

NetWare

Name given to Novell's line of Network Operating Systems (NOS) for dedicated servers.

Network adapter, network card

A network adapter is a card inserted in one of the PC's slots and connected to the network cabling on the other end. Different cards and often different interconnection hardwares are required depending on the type of network used (Ethernet, Fast Ethernet, Token Ring, ATM, FDDI, etc.).

Network client

A function (service) of the operating system, or a piece of software that enables a PC to connect to the resources (disks, printers, etc.) of another PC.

Network manager

Term used at times to refer to a Network Operating System (NOS).

NIC (Network interface card)

This term refers to network adapters.

NOS

Acronym for Network Operating System (NetWare, Windows NT Server, OS/2 Server, etc.).

Novell

One of the two leading publishers of network operating systems (NOS), notably NetWare.

Paradiaphony

A defect in a network cable that 'mixes up' signals going through its twisted pairs. There is always some paradiaphony in a network cable, but it is negligible in good quality cables.

Peer-to-peer network

A network where every PC can be a server or a client or both. A peer-to-peer network is economical, easy to set up, but not very efficient. Windows for Workgroups, Windows 95, Windows 98 and Windows NT WorkStation include a simple peer-to-peer network free of charge.

PPP (Point to Point Protocol)

One of the protocols capable of 'packaging' digital data for transmission by modem. It is now used exclusively by Internet Service Providers.

RAS (Remote Access Services)

A Windows service that enables users of a local area network to connect to that network by means of a modem and a telephone line.

RJ45

Name given to network connectors that use twisted pair cables.

Server

A server is a computer that centralises the sharing of resources. Such a computer is never a client of other machines, as is the case in peer-to-peer mode, but shares its resources with others. It is always specially optimised for its purpose. An operating system and a client-server application should run on this machine.

Shield

In electromagnetic terms, a shield is a very thin sheet of aluminium that surrounds all the cables and thereby protects them from minor external interference.

SMTP (Simple Mail Transfer Protocol)

The basic protocol for sending messages on the Internet. It is complemented by POP-3 (Post Office Protocol 3) for receiving messages. POP-3 unfortunately has a number of shortcomings, and is being progressively replaced by IMAP-4 (Internet Messaging Access Protocol 4).

SNMP (Simple Network Management Protocol)

The most common protocol for the remote management of network devices.

TCP/IP (Transmission Control Protocol/Internet Protocol)

A protocol developed for the Internet which gets data from one network device to another

Telemaintenance

Telemaintenance consists of remotely accessing a **PC** (via the local area network or a modem) in order to carry out maintenance operations or to assist a user. It uses specific telemaintenance software (the best known being **Norton PC Anywhere**). Whoever is using this application can work on the machine as if s/he were actually sitting in front of it.

Terminator

A coaxial connector with a resistor instead of a cable on the end.

Token Ring

A cabling system consisting of 'drawing' a cable from each **PC** to the concentrator that serves as the central hub.

Twisted pairs

Cable composed of groups of wires that are twisted together two by two. This twisting endows the cable with (relative and limited) immunity to electromagnetic interference.

UTP (Unshielded Twisted Pair)

One of the names given to twisted pair cables used for networking.

Index

INDEX